Better Homes and Gardens®

Pool & Spa

PLANNER

Meredith® Books
Des Moines, Iowa

Pool & Spa Planner

Editors: Brian Kramer, Paula Marshall
Contributing Editor: Bill Nolan
Senior Associate Design Director: Mick Schnepf
Designer: David Jordan
Copy Chief: Terri Fredrickson
Copy and Production Editor: Victoria Forlini
Editorial Operations Manager: Karen Schirm
Managers, Book Production: Pam Kvitne, Marjorie J. Schenkelberg, Rick von Holdt
Contributing Copy Editors: Lorraine Ferrell, Shelley Stewart
Contributing Proofreaders: Julie Cahalan, Pamela Elizian, Sue Fetters
Technical Advice and Review: National Spa & Pool Institute
Contributing Field Editors: Betsy Harris, Karen Lidbeck, Sally Mauer, Lisa Mowry
Contributing Photographers: Jim Hedrich, Robert Mauer, Tom McWilliam, Emily Minton
Contributing Illustrator: Robert LaPointe
Indexer: Kathleen Poole
Editorial and Design Assistants: Kaye Chabot, Karen McFadden, Mary Lee Gavin

Meredith® Books

Editor in Chief: Linda Raglan Cunningham
Design Director: Matt Strelecki
Executive Editor, Home Decorating and Design: Denise L. Caringer

Publisher: James D. Blume
Executive Director, Marketing: Jeffrey Myers
Executive Director, New Business Development: Todd M. Davis
Executive Director, Sales: Ken Zagor
Director, Operations: George A. Susral
Director, Production: Douglas M. Johnston
Business Director: Jim Leonard

Vice President and General Manager: Douglas J. Guendel

Better Homes and Gardens® **Magazine**

Editor in Chief: Karol DeWulf Nickell

Meredith Publishing Group

President, Publishing Group: Stephen M. Lacy
Vice President-Publishing Director: Bob Mate

Meredith Corporation

Chairman and Chief Executive Officer: William T. Kerr

In Memoriam: E. T. Meredith III (1933–2003)

All of us at Better Homes and Gardens® Books are dedicated to providing you with information and ideas to enhance your home. We welcome your comments and suggestions. Write to us at: Better Homes and Gardens Books, Home Decorating and Design Editorial Department, 1716 Locust St., Des Moines, IA 50309-3023.

If you would like to purchase any of our home decorating and design, cooking, crafts, gardening, or home improvement books, check wherever quality books are sold. Or visit us at: bhgbooks.com

Cover Photograph: Ed Gohlich

OFFICIALLY WITHDRAWN

DIVING BOARDS FALL OUT OF FAVOR

Once considered standard equipment for residential pools, diving boards are now found mainly at public pools. Only about 10 percent of new residential pools are designed and equipped to accommodate diving. One reason is that diving boards pose a serious safety hazard when used improperly. Another reason is that safe diving, even from a low board, requires a pool depth of at least 8 feet—and 10 to 12 feet is better. Besides posing a hazard for nonswimmers, the extra depth makes it more difficult to clean the pool and to keep the water heated at an even, comfortable temperature. Also, the extra depth isn't needed for swimming and becomes a hindrance for group activities. As a result, the depth of most pools today ranges from 3 to 5 feet.

Above: Dedicated swimmers enjoy the straight and narrow confines of this kind of lap pool; steps descend into the water in a pointed extention to avoid obstructing the swimming lane.

Escaping to a Private World

Something about still water, whether a pool, pond, or lake, promotes contemplation and reflection and provides a downshift from busy days. If you like to spend your leisure time enjoying quiet interludes in a secluded spot that feels insulated from the cares of the world, you may want to build that kind of ambience into your pool area.

As with other types of design, a private-hideaway pool can be modest in scale and inexpensive, more elaborate and higher priced, or anywhere in between. Also, it can be quite formal and elegant or delightfully informal and whimsical. Two characteristics they all share, however—in addition to the pool, of course—are a sense of enclosure or self-containment and a feeling of repose. If you have a big yard, you can use trees and shrubs to gain enclosure and a broad sweep of lawn to express serenity and simplicity. In a smaller yard, the enclosure might be a high garden wall, with pavers and artfully placed plantings lending order and balance.

The examples shown here are informal in character, resembling ponds in a natural clearing or meadow. Each includes a pool large enough and deep enough for swimming, yet the pools seem more like focal points for quiet meditation than arenas for recreation, exercise, or entertaining. Some people find simply sitting by the water and watching a breeze ripple the surface just as refreshing as taking a dip.

Dual-function pools

With clever planning, you can probably combine key features from each type of pool

discussed in this chapter and create a hybrid that meets your needs even on those occasions when you feel like switching gears. For instance, tucking a small, picturesque outbuilding into your pool area hideaway provides an inconspicuous spot for a cooking area, which will prove handy when you entertain large groups in an outdoor setting. Or a pool used primarily for swimming laps can easily double as a formal reflecting pool, adding an element of symmetry and order to your landscape scheme.

Above: Natural stone paving and a magnificent view of the surrounding terrain lend a rugged beauty to this peaceful scene. Underwater lighting creates a dramatic counterpoint to the darkening sky.

Left: Circular steps near the waterfall seem to have been carved out naturally by the water itself. They offer a spot to sit and savor the peace of the pool's pastoral setting.

Backyard Oases

Creating a private Shangri-la in your backyard doesn't necessarily require a lot of land. These examples show how a pool can fit snugly in a relatively small yard. One tucks into a back corner; the other nudges against the base of a hill. Both offer ideas you can use for achieving a sense of serene detachment from the everyday world—even if that world lies only a few feet away.

Hideaway pool/spa

Ruggedly straight lines and planes lend the modest-size pool/spa, below, an Asian simplicity that complements and contrasts with the lush foliage hugging the hillside above it. The dense greenery provides a strong sense of enclosure, while the pool's clean, crisp shape establishes a soul-soothing sense of repose. These effects are amplified by subtle refinements that become noticeable only as the mind begins to relax and take in small details. One such detail is the artful arrangement of chunks of natural stone, which provides textural relief for the cleanly sculpted walls and deck of the pool. Another is the shallow reveal at the waterline, giving the pool walls a floating effect and emphasizing the horizontal lines that soothe by relating strongly to the earth. To reinforce the simplicity of the space, furnishings are lean and spare, and the only splashes of color—other than the pool itself—are pockets of blooming annuals.

Curtained with cascades

Horizontal lines and planes also play a key role in the design of the L-shape lap pool/spa, opposite. The pool steps, brick deck, and multitiered waterfalls rise out of the water in a graceful topography of thin layers. In addition to relaxing the mind with its earth-anchored horizontals and its broad curtain of gently gurgling cascades,

Below: This secluded pool and spa nestles into a steep slope just outside the back door. Carving a spot into the base of the hill and merging retaining walls and planters with the pool structure nets a grottolike hideaway as private and isolated as a walled courtyard.

Left: Although occupying little more space than a narrow planting bed, this L-shape oasis offers three different antidotes for the stressed-out psyche: lap swimming, a soak in the spa, and the gentle sound of water tumbling down a pair of stairstepped cascades. Below: The longer cascade forms a privacy wall along the rear lot line; the shorter one serves as a spillway for the spa. Dark blue tiles on both cascading waterfalls match those forming the visible center stripe in the lap pool.

the waterfall doubles as a privacy screen, working with the adjoining stucco wall to create a sense of enclosure. Here, as in the hillside pool, opposite, the main color accent is deep blue, which has a decidedly calming effect on most people.

POOL & SPA POINTERS

Never underestimate the soothing effect of natural outdoor sounds, such as a waterfall or a gurgling brook where shallow water runs over rocks. When planning a water feature as part of your pool, incorporate running water to simulate sounds you find relaxing. Connect the pump to a switch that lets you turn it off too.

It's easy for guests to get into a festive mood at this party-perfect pool/spa in Texas. The owners, who love to host casual gatherings outdoors, have made their backyard pool a major focus of their social life by incorporating a broad range of features that handle a crowd easily and make guests feel welcome. The plan they adopted for their project offers several lessons for anyone planning to use their pool area as an entertainment area.

One easy-to-spot feature is the generously sized deck curving gracefully around the pool on all sides. Near the house, it broadens in several places to accommodate multiple seating and dining areas, all within a short stroll of the outdoor kitchen. On the far side of the pool, the deck narrows and nestles against the terraced hillside, providing sheltered areas for lounging and sunbathing.

Another prominent feature is the picturesque rock waterfall that tumbles into the pool from the hillside. The landslide-style placement of rocks and small boulders creates a rustic cascade that contrasts dramatically with the graceful curves of the pool's edge. A second waterfall flanks the spa at the far end of the pool, and the spa itself sports an elegant central fountain. Together, these features lend an element of theater that adds to the pool's festive mood and makes guests feel transported to another world.

In addition to several umbrella-topped tables, outdoor seating includes a covered area outfitted with ceiling fans—an especially useful amenity in locales where cooling breezes can be scarce. At night—usually the most comfortable time to be outdoors in the Texas summers— the entire pool area can be illuminated with large stainless-steel tiki torches.

Although the pool area merges almost seamlessly with its setting and appears to be lushly landscaped, most of the permanent plantings are confined to the terraced hillside and the narrow beds at its base. Large pots of annuals are placed strategically for local color and require little care. This tactic clears the deck—literally—for partying and gives the owners more free time to enjoy the pool themselves.

Opposite: What was nothing more than a flat, empty stretch of brown grass all summer long is now a lush, resortlike oasis. The generous-size pool seems to be fed by a rocky cascade that tumbles down the hill on one side. Stone coping frames the pool in a series of elegant arcs that lead the eye toward a fountain and spa at the far end. Although the pool shape appears irregular, it's long and straight enough for lap swimming.

Right: A guaranteed crowd-pleaser, the integral spa at this backyard pool features broad stone ledges curving around a central fountain. Nearby, water cascades over rocks and boulders into the pool. At dusk, tiki torches set the pool area aglow.

Left: Near the large waterfall, sunbathers can perch on a reef—a ledge only a few inches underwater—to keep cool. Above: This pool also has a hidden asset: Instead of treating the water with chlorine, the pool's circulation system uses salt tablets to generate the chlorine naturally. This method eliminates the odor prevalent in chlorine-treated pools.

Multilevel Family Fun

Below: Stairstepping the pool and deck in this hillside backyard tamed the slope and made it easier to supervise children splashing in the pool or playing on the lawn below.

Narrow, downhill lots may seem unlikely places to install full-size pools with spas, but this example shows how smart design can meet the challenge. The owners spend lots of time outdoors with their children—and with friends who also have children—so they wanted to give their pool area as much livability as possible. At the same time, they wanted to preserve part of their yard as a playground and lawn area, one they could easily supervise from the pool or spa. Their pool designer developed a multilevel scheme that could adapt to any snug site, whether on a gentle grade or a fairly steep one.

One key to the designer's hill-taming strategy is the infinity-edge pool (for more about this unusual feature, turn to page 116), which doubles as a retaining wall and also as a waterfall between the pool area and the playground. The pool and spa are located at the top of the hill, close to the house. A multilevel, stone-paved terrace forms the pool deck and wraps around the spa. One end of the terrace extends several feet under an airy trellis to provide room for an outdoor kitchen and dining area. A few steps down is a circular fire pit where moms and dads can warm their toes and sit comfortably while they watch the kids take an evening dip or have a final romp on the playground.

The pool itself is roughly rectangular with pool steps tucked into one side between stone piers, providing an ample amount of water for splashing around and playing games. The spa is slightly higher, making it easy to keep an eye on the kids in the pool while soaking.

Top Left: Blue tiles, such as those on the spa, add a splash of color to the pool's infinity edge. Here, pool runoff forms a waterfall that ties the pool area to the lower yard. Part of the runoff returns to the pool via a picturesque, boulder-strewn cascade (visible in the background).

Bottom Left: Azure blue ceramic tiles form a broad spillway for sheets of water that slide over the edge of the spa and empty into the pool. The deep hue of the tiles echoes the color of the pool itself.

Building Within Your Budget

Will your dream pool fit your real-life pocketbook? Here's how to make sure—before you take the plunge.

Adding a pool is a major home improvement, comparable in cost to adding on a new room, updating a kitchen or bath, or upgrading your home's exterior. But like all such improvements, a pool project can be tailored to fit a broad range of budgets because pools come in several different price categories, each offering a wide array of design options.

If a major concern is staying within a strict budget, do your homework up front before zeroing in on a specific pool package. Becoming familiar with each type of pool product and knowing all the options ahead of time will save you money in the long run. Another way to avoid sticker shock is to do part of the work yourself. But keep in mind that most pool installations require skilled labor and special tools and machinery; don't count on sweat equity to cover a significant portion of the work unless you choose a DIY-friendly pool design.

A third strategy, one that may keep you in the black regardless of pool type, is to develop a long-range plan to create your backyard water wonderland in a series of affordable phases or stages. This chapter gives you a head start on number crunching by taking a closer look at each of these strategies.

Installing this pool partially above ground lessened the need for excavation, which can be one of the more costly factors in building a pool, depending on the underlying soil or rocks. This rectangular pool tucks neatly into an L-shape space with a covered portico for dining and relaxing at one end. Neat brick pavers complement the traditional architecture of the house, and a ledge along the top of the pool wall offers extra seating.

Pool Types

Aboveground

For many years, aboveground pools have maintained a well-deserved reputation for being budget-friendly. Even though prices in all categories have crept steadily upward during the past few decades, aboverounds still offer a lot of pool for the money.

Prices start at about $3,000 for a basic round pool measuring 24 feet in diameter and 4 feet deep. If you need more room to splash around, you can buy a larger-diameter round pool or an oval 12×18-foot pool for under $5,000. Even when they contain approximately the same square footage as a round pool, ovals seem roomier because their shape is more rectangular. However, they cost more to erect and take up more space.

Better looking, more durable

If you haven't looked at aboveground pools for several years, you're in for some pleasant surprises. The old cattle tank look has given way to a new generation of aboverounds that are sleeker and more durable and that offer a wide range of upgrade options. Once considered a temporary solution at best, aboverounds are now gaining acceptance among consumers as a long-term, fairly permanent type of pool installation. Originally, aboveground pools were constructed much like watering tanks, with walls of galvanized steel. Steel is still used widely but with special finishes, such as galvanized, to improve durability, and decorative coatings to give it a subtle, up-to-date look that blends in with the landscape. Some manufacturers have switched to solid resin walls, which consist of interlocking components formed in molds at high temperatures. Besides being rustproof, resin components are colored throughout, so their finish never wears off. These new finishes are available in a number of nature-friendly colors, including gray, blue, beige, tan, and cream.

New, improved pool packages

Until recently, all aboveground pools needed buttresses to support the pool walls. The buttresses extended about 3 feet from the sides of the pool, adding to the amount of yard space required. Some pool manufacturers now offer zero-buttress aboverounds with structural components engineered to provide the required support. Also, above-

Pool Prices

Aboveground pool prices are fairly constant coast to coast, whereas inground pool prices vary according to type and region. Ingrounds cost more in colder climates and areas that are earthquake-prone.

BASIC POOL TYPE	WEST COAST	SUNBELT	SNOWBELT
Aboveground	$3,000–5,000	$3,000–5,000	$3,000–5,000
Vinyl-lined	$20,000–30,000	$15,000–25,000	$15,000–25,000
Fiberglass	$25,000–35,000	$20,000–30,000	$20,000–30,000
Concrete	$50,000–100,000	$15,000–30,000	$25,000–50,000

grounds are now available with taller walls. In older models, the standard wall height was 48 inches, with 40-inch water depth. Newer, 58-inch versions allow an additional 10 inches of water depth.

Abovegrounds now come with better quality equipment, including higher-horsepower pumps and well-engineered, longer-lasting filter systems. There's a new look inside these pools, as well. Several companies now offer vinyl liners featuring tile patterns above the waterline to mimic liners and real tile finishes in their inground cousins. And unlike their bare-bones predecessors, today's abovegrounds can be upgraded with a wide array of accessories to rival those found in more costly inground pools.

One such option is special lighting, both underwater and perimeter types. The perimeter category includes fiber optic lighting, a relatively new type only recently adapted for inground pools. (For more on fiber optics, see page 119.) Other add-ons include designer top railings and access stairs, as well as automatic pool cleaners and chlorine generators.

New options, such as railings, decking, and wood surrounds, make aboveground pools just as functional and attractive as any inground pool. The stylish deck and bench on this pool provide seating right at water level, so keeping any eye on children in the pool is easier.

Swimming in Style—Above Ground

Who says the least-expensive pool installations have to look second-rate? Here are two attractive examples that offer convincing evidence to the contrary. Each is large enough to accommodate activities such as swimming, team sports, and shallow diving. Each also boasts a generous amount of deck space for sunning, sitting, and poolside lounging.

At first glance, each appears to be an inground pool. Both, however, are above the ground. Choosing the simple shapes, factory-production economies, and easy-assembly features offered by aboveground pools saved these homeowners several thousand dollars in initial costs. This gave them more leeway to splurge on extras such as wood decks and railings, attractive retaining walls, and a comfy arbor/swing seating area, to make their pools look more like

those in the ground. Additional savings can be realized by constructing the decks and railings with do-it-yourself skills rather than hiring carpenters. In each case the designs are basic enough that an experienced do-it-yourselfer can duplicate them quite readily.

In general, a flat site is recommended for aboveground pools because they need to be erected on ground that's perfectly level. However, it's more difficult to achieve an inground look on flat sites, and sloping sites actually offer interesting opportunities to camouflage the pool's walls—if, that is, you're willing and able to do some serious digging or can afford to hire it done. Take, for example, the rectangular pool below, which looks like inground installation—one end burrows into the sloping site. Part of the hill has been cut back to create a level area for erecting the pool walls, which

Below: Nosing one end of this elegantly simple aboveground pool into the hillside helped give it the look of an expensive inground installation. While excavating for the pool walls, the work crew dug that end deeper so that it can be used for shallow diving and a water slide.

Left: Although its price falls toward the low end of the scale, this aboveground pool has features that older models didn't have. Most noticeable are the crisp white railing, an attached deck at pool level, and a green finish that blends with the landscape. Even more important, the pool has no buttress supports around the edges—it takes up less room in the yard and the base can be filled in with plantings.

include 3-foot-wide buttresses spaced at regular intervals. The deck bridges the excavated area needed for the buttresses and merges the pool with the hillside. Manufactured-stone retaining walls hold back the hill along the edges of the deck and form attractive planters.

The example above illustrates an even easier way to take advantage of a sloping site. Here, less excavation was required because the aboveground pool is incorporated into a main-level deck, creating an inground look even though the pool walls are mostly above grade. Skirting (not shown) under the deck camouflages the pool walls and encloses the rest of the under-deck area so it can be used for storing pool equipment and garden tools.

POOL & SPA POINTERS

The one thing no one should ever do is dive into an aboveground pool; it's just not deep enough. To remind everyone who uses the pool about this safety concern, be sure to post a "No Diving" sign on or near the pool.

Below: In this cross-section view, you can see how a relatively flat yard can be recontoured to create the look of an inground pool using an aboveground style.

Pool Types

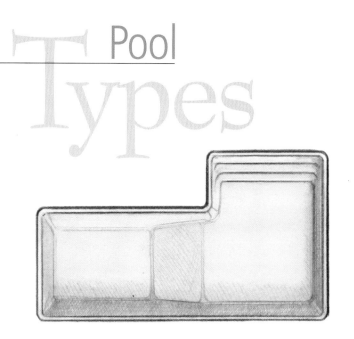

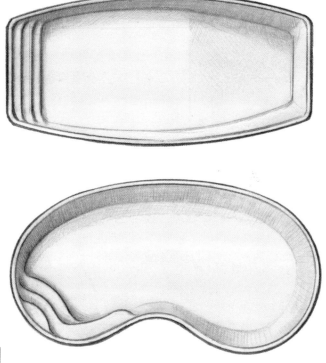

Above: The variety of shapes in ready-to-order, vinyl-lined pools is nearly limitless. When making your selection, keep in mind that the simpler-shape liners are less expensive to fabricate and less likely to be damaged during installation.

Vinyl-Lined

Although inground pools tend to be more expensive than above grounds, they do include at least a few slim-budget options. The three most common types of ingrounds are the vinyl-lined pool, the fiberglass pool, and the concrete pool. Of these, the vinyl-lined is generally the most affordable, with fiberglass pools a close second, particularly if you're comparing ingrounds of similar shape and size. Both types are factory-produced for quick installation on-site, whereas concrete pools are built from scratch on each site, using skilled labor.

One significant advantage of a vinyl-lined pool is that it looks very much like a custom-built pool once it's installed. Another advantage is that you can get virtually any shape, from a simple rectangle to an elaborate free-form or amoeba shape. Keep in mind, however, that prices escalate sharply for more complex shapes.

The cost of a fully installed, simple, rectangular, vinyl-lined 16×32-foot pool with a 4-foot-wide deck on three sides and a 6-foot-wide deck at one end is about $25,000. This figure includes all of the equipment needed to operate the pool, but doesn't include landscaping, fencing, lighting, or other perimeter improvements.

Switching to a more complicated pool shape, adding a host of special amenities, and installing an elaborate landscaping scheme could easily double the price. It's possible to purchase a vinyl-lined pool kit for about $15,000 and install it yourself. If, however, you run into snags, local dealers or pool contractors may not be willing to troubleshoot problems on products they don't handle regularly.

Quick installation

Another advantage of vinyl-lined pools is that, like the abovegrounds, they can be installed quickly. Once the pool arrives from the factory and a crew is available to begin work, your pool can be ready for that first swim in less than a week. Completion may take several days or weeks longer if your backyard poses challenges regarding access, soil conditions, slopes, or other special circumstances.

Properly installed, a vinyl-lined pool will last for many years. Reputable dealers usually offer a lifetime warranty on their pool walls and steps and from 10 to 30 years on their liners. Liners usually need to be replaced once every 10 to 15 years because they're prone to damage from punctures, unbalanced water chemistry, and long-term exposure to ultraviolet light. However, replacing a liner is a relatively simple and

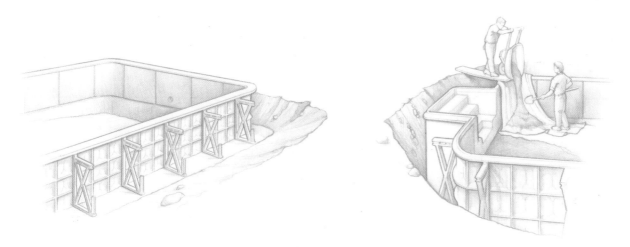

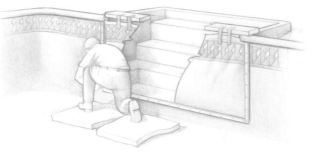

Left: Construction of a vinyl-lined pool usually takes less than a week and involves 6 basic steps: 1) Excavation. 2) Erection of walls and pouring of bond beam. 3) Pouring of floor and installation of drains and skimmers. 4) Installation of liner. 5) Filling of pool and backfilling of excavation. 6) Pouring of deck.

inexpensive task—and the result is a pool that looks brand-new.

New bells and whistles

Not long ago, owners of vinyl-lined pools had few choices for upgrading or embellishing their pool package. Now options are almost as varied as those for custom-built concrete pools. In addition to premolded recessed stair units, many vinyl-lined pools can be outfitted with reefs, integral spas, waterfalls, and fountains. A few models even come with an infinity edge (also called a vanishing edge or negative edge). If you need a vinyl-lined pool in a special shape (for instance, to fit an existing pool you're rehabbing), you can custom-order a vinyl liner to meet your requirements—in some cases your order will be filled and shipped in just a few days.

Making a Big Splash with Vinyl-Lined

Compared to other types of ingrounds, the vinyl-lined pool may be the most affordable option, but it doesn't have to look ho-hum. Vinyl-lined pools are nearly as versatile and adaptable as their concrete or fiberglass counterparts. The pools on these pages demonstrate two of the many design possibilities. Although any pool becomes costly when you choose an unusual shape or add special features such as a waterfall, a spa, or a natural stone deck, the money you save by going vinyl will help offset the costs of these extras.

Urbane suburban

A vinyl-lined pool lends itself to the drama and elegance of classic geometric shapes just as easily as to free-form informality. The pool below makes a striking design statement by combining dramatically angled sidewalls with symmetrically curved ends. This artful interplay isn't just for looks; angling the side walls segregates the diving end from the shallow end, and the curved areas give swimmers and bathers places to congregate. Note the placement of the spa near the shallow end, where adults can soak while they supervise small-fry swimmers.

Country casual

Reminiscent of an old mill pond—complete with waterfall—the free-form pool opposite looks comfortably at home in its tree-lined setting. The meandering stone deck and the lazy curves of the pool and retaining wall put you in a relaxed frame of mind even before you take a dip. A quaintly styled arbor, a copper-roofed birdhouse, and a stone birdbath accentuate the pool's simple, down-home charm.

This rustic character would actually be a bit costly to duplicate—mainly because of the unusually complex shape of the pool and the extensive use of natural stone. If your budget has room for an inground pool but a definite limit on the number of extras you

Below: Deep shades of blue in this pool/spa are set off by rich earth tones in the interlocking pavers and brick coping that form the deck. Although the pool is vinyl-lined and the spa is concrete finished in blue tile, the two work together as a unified design.

If you love a certain surface but feel it's too expensive, does that mean you shouldn't use it? Not at all! Simply use it wisely, where it's most effective, and you can use anything you like. For instance, if brick is too costly for the whole deck, design a concrete deck surrounded with a brick edging. Or insert 6×6-foot sections of brick pavers at the corners of the deck, using them as bases for pots of flowering plants.

can include, consider building a less expensive version by making a few strategic changes. For instance, choosing a simpler free-form shape could save you several hundred dollars without noticeably diminishing the overall effect. And going with cultured stone or salvaged pavers can net additional savings. Also, you can add the curvy wall and the waterfall later as funds become available.

Above: Dressed-stone coping and cobbled pavers give this vinyl-lined pool its unique character. One side rises an extra 3 feet to form a curving planter and a waterfall. The planter leads the eye to the Victorian-style arbor and stone bench at the far end of the pool.

Pool Types

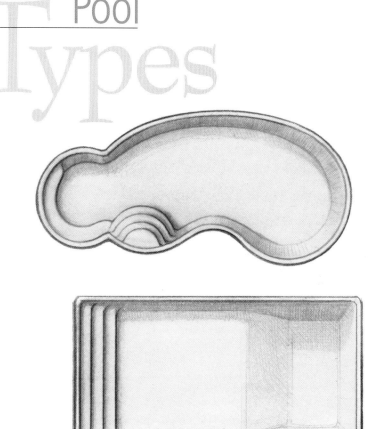

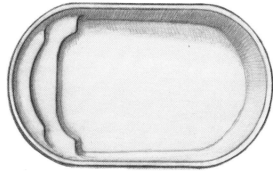

Fiberglass

Somewhat higher priced than the average vinyl-lined pool yet still offering the cost advantages of factory production, fiberglass pools are a good choice if you want long-term durability but can't afford a built-from-scratch concrete pool. A fiberglass pool is manufactured as a one-piece shell, so there is no liner to replace. The finish color is an integral part of the shell, not troweled or painted on after installation, so you never need to replaster or repaint. Because this type of pool shell arrives at the site in one piece, it can be installed almost as quickly as a vinyl-lined pool. One disadvantage, however, is that an item as large as a pool can't be easily transported long distances, so you may have difficulty arranging delivery of a fiberglass pool if you live in a remote area.

Advantages and drawbacks

Developed as a spin-off of the fiberglass boat industry in the late 1950s, the fiberglass pool is a relative newcomer that is quickly carving out a niche for itself in the American residential pool market. Ease of maintenance is one of the primary reasons for its rapid acceptance. The outer surface of the shell is a layer of nonporous, inert, gel-coat resin bonded permanently to the fiberglass. This finish is so smooth algae won't stick to it. It's also highly resistant to acids and oxidants (common ingredients in pool chemicals) and to ultraviolet radiation. However, because it scratches easily, be careful not to put sharp objects in the pool or use abrasive cleaners to remove the bathtub ring (deposits from oils and lotions that form a line of scum at the waterline).

Another advantage of fiberglass shells is that once they are installed and filled with water, they are unusually strong—17 times stronger than concrete and considerably more resilient. They are an excellent choice for areas where soil pressures, soil shifts, or seismic disturbances are a concern.

Although installation involves relatively few steps compared to those of a concrete pool, it's not a project easily handled by amateurs. The area to be excavated needs to be sized and shaped very carefully to match the bottom of the shell, and the shell itself needs to be unloaded and placed with a large crane, then leveled properly before being filled. Once in position, the narrow void between the shell and excavation must be filled with watered sand at the same time the pool is filled to equalize the pressure on the shell, or it will fracture. The whole operation must take place during calm, dry weather; when lifting a shell with a crane,

even a light wind can be hazardous, and an unfilled shell could be damaged by becoming buoyant and shifting out of plumb in a sudden rainstorm.

Like other types of ingrounds, fiberglass pools come with long-term warranties. Most manufacturers offer at least a 25-year warranty on the pool shell. Some offer 35 years or even a lifetime warranty. Warranties on other components, such as pumps and filters, are generally the same as those for vinyl-lined or concrete pools.

Stainless-steel pools

A close cousin of the fiberglass pool is the stainless-steel pool. Like fiberglass, stainless steel arrives at the site prefinished and doesn't require a liner or on-site finishing, so installation can be done quickly. But stainless-steel pools tend to be smaller, simpler shapes, and they usually cost more than fiberglass units of comparable size.

Left: A fiberglass pool arrives at the site in one piece and is lifted into place with a crane. After it's leveled, the pool shell is filled with water and the ground around the exterior is backfilled with sand to lock it in place. Then a concrete deck is poured around the rim.

Concrete Inground

Above: To build a concrete pool, workers set forms and line the excavation with steel rebar, then spray gunite or shotcrete inside the forms to create a specified wall and floor thickness. Care is taken to eliminate air pockets, which could weaken the concrete. When it has cured, the concrete is sprayed with pressurized water to expose the aggregate in the concrete mix and painted or given a finish coat of smooth plaster, marcite, or ceramic tile.

Once the only type of inground pool, concrete is still considered by many owners and builders to be the best option overall. Like fiberglass, concrete offers long-term durability and almost unlimited freedom of design. When constructed properly, a concrete shell may last several decades and if it has a high-performance finish, it may not ever require anything except routine maintenance.

Because concrete is a much heavier material than fiberglass, metal, or polymers, all concrete pools are still built from scratch on-site rather than shipped as precast units. (This may change if a form of lightweight concrete is developed for prefab pool manufacture.) Although site-built pools are more labor intensive and considerably more expensive than factory-built versions, there are ways to economize.

One tactic is to keep the pool shape as simple as possible: A rectangle or modified L shape is much cheaper to build than a free-form shape. Another tactic is to avoid costly finish materials or to use them sparingly to create the most dramatic effect.

Many budget-minded pool owners opt for a painted or plastered finish below the waterline with a decorative tile border above, where it can be easily seen; this combination is much less expensive, although somewhat less durable, than lining the entire pool with tile.

Building from scratch also gives you the freedom to custom-fit your pool to your backyard and to place special features, such as steps, ledges, and a spa, exactly where you want them. If your pool site poses structural challenges, such as unstable soil conditions or a steep slope, site-built concrete structures can usually be engineered to handle the problem—for a price, of course.

Most concrete pools are constructed with a special concrete mix (either gunite or shotcrete) that's pressure-sprayed into place and reinforced with steel bars (rebar). Where extra strength is needed, more steel and thicker walls, piers, and footings are used. As the sides and floor of the pool take shape, the surfaces are troweled to eliminate irregularities. After the concrete cures, the surfaces are given a decorative finish. The least expensive finishes are paint and exposed aggregate. A little more expensive but much more popular are plaster and marcite (a plasterlike coating made with powdered marble). Of these finishes, the exposed aggregate is the most durable because it doesn't peel or chip like paint or eventually crack like troweled-on finishes. Aggregates are somewhat bumpy or pebbly, however, whereas plaster and marcite are relatively smooth.

New formula finishes

Until recently, the preferred finish choice for top-of-the-line concrete pools was ceramic tile, but newer high-performance finishes have begun to win converts among pool owners, especially in the Sunbelt. Some of these new finishes are smoothly polished to resemble tile and plaster; others are more pebbly like aggregates. Most have been formulated to provide denser, less porous surfaces that resist staining and many of them incorporate beads of colored glass or stone for camouflage.

The shell for this naturalistic pool/spa is concrete, a good choice for constructing irregular shapes because each concrete pool is a one-of-a-kind design built from scratch at the site. Here, large natural stone accents with stone decking, coping, and steps blend the pool and spa seamlessly into their leafy setting.

Investing in Quality: Concrete or Fiberglass

If your budget is fairly ample and if long-term durability and optimum flexibility in design are primary objectives, then you may want to invest in a concrete or fiberglass pool. The ability of both of these materials to deliver a high standard of structural strength and to express virtually any shape imaginable makes them the top choices among many pool designers and homeowners.

Nestled among the boulders

Building from scratch with concrete offers you the chance to let your imagination run wild. The free-form pool/spa, right, demonstrates concrete's almost limitless possibilities by creating a magical place that usually exists only in imaginations. The shape of the pool seems totally random and nestles among boulders at the foot of a rock outcropping as if tucked away on a tropical island, just waiting to be discovered. The waterfall and spa, a lush carpet of ground-cover, and a curtain of exotic greenery amplify the pool's fantastical qualities. Although a pool this complex would be quite expensive, money ordinarily used for decking could be diverted to pay for other features that make this design so unique. Also, using tinted and scored concrete instead of cut stone for the paving is another way in which this design holds the line on costs.

Imagination played a key role in shaping this unique pool—and so did concrete. What appear to be cut-stone rims and a curvy path meandering among tawny boulders are actually concrete, including the free-form boulders. If you're willing to pay the price, skilled masons can likely craft your dream pool in concrete too.

STONE—NATURE'S ARTISTIC EXPRESSION

Mother Nature is undoubtedly the finest artist there is. Every piece of natural stone—whether cut from a quarry or deposited by a long-ago glacier—has unique character with a shape and markings like no other. (Simulated stones, such as those above, imitate nature's artistry and often come amazingly close.) But where can you find real rocks? Most large towns have landscaping companies that sell boulders by weight. In colder climates, frost heaves stones out of the fields every winter, and farmers are usually glad to get rid of them.

Using interesting rocks and large boulders around a pool brings a feeling of permanence and stability to the setting, but there are guidelines for using them well. If possible, obtain local rocks compatible with the terrain in your area. Choose them for their shape and color, avoiding soft, sedimentary types that are apt to separate into layers. Plan to have at least one larger rock and several smaller ones in each grouping. To make the rocks look like natural outcroppings, bury the lower portion in the soil (or below the surface of the deck), leaving about three-fourths above ground level.

Planning Phases 1

Developing a Plan

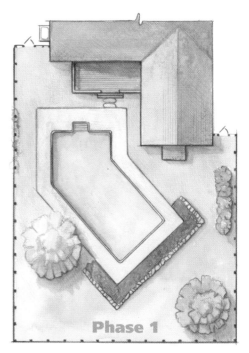

Phase 1

Nearly any permanently installed pool involves a major investment, one that merits careful planning. This is especially important if you're on a strict budget yet want your dream backyard pool. Like any sizable home improvement project, a pool will likely cost more than you first thought, but a detailed plan helps head off unpleasant surprises and setbacks. Also, doing the work in stages over a period of several years helps spread the financial load and offers the opportunity to fine-tune the design of the pool area as you live with it. For these and other reasons, it's smart to develop a long-range master plan with several phases, even if you have the resources to do the whole project in a single season.

Start the planning process by compiling a list of must-have features for the pool itself, the adjoining activity or lounging areas, the landscaping, and the perimeter. Cover the basic necessities, such as items needed for safety, security, and routine maintenance, and include a few splurges—items that will give your pool extra convenience and livability—even if you

aren't able to build them right away.

After honing your list to a manageable size, crunch the numbers. Talk to dealers and contractors, and nail down what each item will cost; then take another hard look at your list. Should anything be eliminated? Which items should get priority? Look for ways to do some of the labor yourself, and figure those savings into the mix.

Another advantage of long-term planning is that you can postpone some big-ticket expenses and substitute low-cost alternatives until you can afford to upgrade. Inexpensive welded-wire fencing around the pool, for example, will meet basic safety requirements if installed with sturdy posts and stringers. You can upgrade later by replacing it with wooden planks or wrought-iron spokes. And the spot for a future spa can temporarily serve as a planting bed, a sandbox, or a fire pit until you're ready. Let Mother Nature help with your long-term plan too. Buy small, inexpensive trees and shrubs, and plant them the first year so they can start growing right away. Until they are larger, fill in with annuals or easy-to-transplant perennials.

Once your list is finalized, the next step is to get your ideas down on paper and see how they compare with other factors that need to be addressed, such as local codes and regulations, climatic conditions, and privacy concerns. To bring matters into focus, draw up a site plan and a plot plan of your property (see pages 38–41) and use those as

Below: Perfect symmetry is obvious in this classically proportioned pool and elegant deck. Nevertheless, it could be built in stages, with the pool coming first, the deck and spa next, and brick walls and outbuildings later.

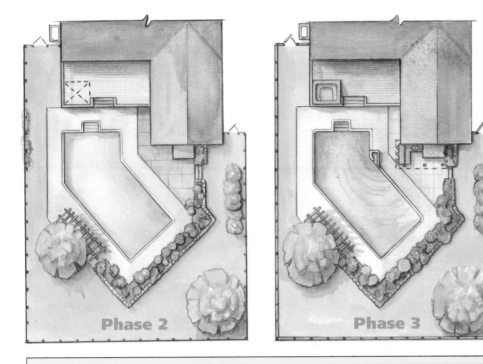

Phase 2   Phase 3

Left: These drawings illustrate how a pool and its surrounding landscape can come about in stages. Compare them carefully to see how various extra features are added over time, realizing that the pool itself is usable from the very beginning.

DOING IT IN PHASES: BUDGET BREAKDOWN

PHASE ONE
- Install vinyl-lined inground pool and 4-foot concrete deck $25,000
- Install temporary perimeter fence; plant with vines for quick privacy ....$ 1,000
- Build small storage shed next to house for pool equipment ....$ 500
- Plant grass seed; lay out and mulch future beds for perennials ....$ 100
- Plant trees and shrubs that will be used for shade and privacy screens ....$ 2,000
- Buy umbrella table ....$ 100
- Install basic pool alarms ....$ 100

PHASE TWO
- Build a pergola or gazebo ....$ 3,000
- Enlarge the deck for seating; leave an open square for future spa ....$ 3,000
- Plant filler trees and shrubs ....$ 1,500
- Add basic outdoor lighting ....$ 600
- Enlarge pool deck to create dining/sunning terrace and add seating area near the pergola ...$ 5,000
- Plant perennials in mulched beds along pool's edge ....$ 2,000

PHASE THREE
- Expand storage shed into outdoor kitchen and cabana ....$ 5,000
- Install fiberglass or concrete spa; build skirting to match pool deck ....$ 7,000
- Upgrade perimeter fencing with wooden louver sections and gates ....$ 2,000
- Add a fountain or waterfall ....$ 500
- Upgrade the lighting with fiber optics and an automatic control system ....$ 2,600
- Install automatic pool cleaner ....$ 4,000
- Install automatic pool cover ....$ 9,000

the basis for drawing up a multiphase master plan. To make the most of your space and budget, consider enlisting the help of a pool designer and/or landscape architect as you develop your plan. Putting your own stamp on the design is very important. You want a pool that fits your family's lifestyle, not someone else's abstract notion of style and beauty.

The plan above is a typical example. Keep in mind that a master plan is a guideline and not a rule book. As you complete each phase, you may discover additional ways to fine-tune your plan.

Construction Basics

Building a Pool

SITE PLAN CHECKLIST

- Lot lines: Draw on graph paper and notate the length of each.
- Setbacks: Indicate with dotted lines and show distance from lot lines.
- House: Draw to scale and show exact location on lot.
- Easements: Indicate with dotted lines and describe with a note.
- Existing structures: Draw to scale and describe with notes; label "keep" or "remove."
- Existing landscaping: Indicate type and location; label "keep" or "remove."
- Overhead obstructions: Indicate with heavy dotted lines and label; note vertical clearance on low-hanging obstructions.
- Underground obstructions: Indicate with dotted lines (long dashes) and describe with note; label "keep" or "remove."
- Shady areas: Indicate with shaded pencil strokes; show main morning shade area(s) and main afternoon shade area(s).
- Prevailing winds: Indicate with solid lines and arrows and label each.
- Utility sources: Indicate location of electrical outlets, hose bibs, light fixtures, phone cables; label each.

Building a pool in your backyard requires careful planning and preparation. Start by developing a detailed concept of what your pool will look like and the features it will include. Also, determine how it will fit into its site and what will be involved or required in its construction.

Most of the concerns you need to address are the same ones that apply to any major residential remodeling project: What local codes and regulations must be followed? Does your backyard pose any special conditions or challenges for the type of pool construction you have in mind? Will your pool's location take full advantage of available views? Will it provide adequate privacy from neighbors? What services should you expect from a pool designer or pool contractor? Reputable pool-industry professionals in your area—designers, builders, dealers, and service providers—can supply a lot of the answers you'll be seeking. But your involvement is important. The more informed you are, the better your decisions.

Sizing up your site

Before you get too far along, factor in the real-life conditions and limitations of your building site. If the pool of your dreams is too big for the space available, the time to find out is now, not when you sit down with a designer or dealer to make a selection. Take exact measurements and draw your lot to scale on a large sheet of graph paper so you have an accurate reference. If your lot is too steep or slopes the wrong direction to provide proper drainage, you may need to rethink your pool's placement or shape as

well as the amount of money you need to set aside for site preparation. Ideally, a pool should be sited on high ground with slightly down-sloping grades on all sides so runoff doesn't drain into the pool. Don't assume that your yard is level; looks can be deceiving. Check it at several points with a long string and a carpenter's level, and record the approximate changes in elevation per foot along the string. (For additional tips regarding terrain, see page 44.) Also, keep in mind that the buildable space in your yard is probably not defined by lot lines. In most communities, residential construction projects are subject to setback restrictions, covenants, and various easements. These regulations are set up to establish a uniform character for the neighborhood, keep adjoining homes and structures from being built too close together, and provide access along

property lines for servicing utilities. To find out what restrictions are in force for your property, visit the recorder's office or zoning and codes official at your local courthouse or city hall and check the legal plat that is on file there for your home. (A copy of the plat should also be in your home's abstract.) Read the fine print on your deed, which is where special restrictions or covenants that apply to lots in your particular neighborhood are listed.

Your site may be hiding other invisible limitations that need to be pinpointed and removed or worked around, such as buried utility lines, drainage culverts, fuel tanks or septic systems, and areas where the original grade has been filled with unstable soil. The

local power and water companies will mark the location of utility lines for you. Talking with longtime residents is often the best way to find out about other surprises that may be hidden underground.

Finally, as you examine your site and record your findings, take note of the microclimate that various natural and artificial influences have created in your backyard. From which directions does the wind blow most often? Are there areas that are protected by existing trees and shrubs, privacy fencing, or your house or garage? Which areas are sunny and which are shady at various times of the day? Do these conditions vary significantly from one season to another?

Properly situating a pool on a sloped lot like this takes planning. It's also an opportunity for some creative thinking. By playing up the curves of the site, the pool becomes an organic part of the landscape.

Codes

Check with these local officials regarding legal restrictions and other regulations when planning a pool.
- County sanitarian or municipal public health officer
- Local power company
- Municipal or rural water system
- Local communications providers
- City or county building department
- City or county clerk's or recorder's office

Before construction begins, your pool project needs to jump through a series of legal hoops involving building codes, health regulations, and other types of laws or ordinances pertaining to residential pools, spas, and outdoor structures. Codes and regulations tend to be more complex and detailed in large urban areas than in small towns or rural areas but when it comes to home improvement projects of this scale, most any residence is subject to some form of regulation. If you're hiring a contractor to do all or most of the work, he or she can handle most of the legal hurdles for you. However, you'd be wise to know what these hurdles are because they may affect the design and cost of your project.

Generally, a pool project requires two kinds of construction permits: a building permit and an electrical permit. These are issued by the building department at your local city hall or county courthouse. To get them, you need to submit detailed plans of your project. Check with your local building department to see what information to include on the plans and how many sets of plans to submit (usually two). Most departments provide a free brochure that answers these questions.

After the permits are issued and construction begins, your project will need to pass a series of inspections. Your contractor will schedule these according to the expected completion of each stage of construction. Passing an inspection is called getting an approval.

Permits are issued if your plans indicate that your project will meet the appropriate building codes. These codes represent the minimum acceptable standards for a given type of construction in your locale. Pool project codes often dictate such things as the size and depth of footings, the thickness of the pool walls (in the case of a concrete pool), and the height of the perimeter fencing. Some codes are universal, but many apply only to a particular locale and can vary widely from city to city or from urban to rural areas.

If you find that your pool plans violate a specific restriction, you may be able to get a

Intricate backyard schemes, like this pool and multilevel deck, require careful planning to take advantage of the lot and to make sure they meet local codes.

variance (official permission to bend the rule to some degree). Variances are often granted by a review board when property owners demonstrate that they would suffer hardships (such as excessive expense) by adhering to certain restrictions. To have your case reviewed, you need to fill out a questionnaire and submit it to the board, then attend a meeting of the board on the day that your request is scheduled for a hearing.

Drawing up a plot plan

Once you've analyzed the site and addressed any applicable legal issues, it's time to begin developing a plot plan. Basically, a plot plan is like a floor plan; it shows the various areas and features that you want to include in your pool project. If you're dividing your project into phases, the plot plan should includes all phases. For the sake of simplicity, however, the first phase can be thought of as the plot plan if it includes most of the major or determining design decisions. Future phases, which may be altered before the project is complete, can be drawn on tracing paper, with new tracing-paper drawings added as the project evolves.

One decision key to your plot plan is the location of your pool. Another is the pool's shape, and a third is its size (overall dimensions). Several factors come into play here, likely already noted in your site plan (see pages 38–39). For instance, unless you live in a hot climate, you'll probably want to place your pool where it will get direct sun most of the day; swimming in the shade can be chilly during mild, dry weather. You may, however, want shade on part of the pool deck during the hottest part of the day. You may also want to orient your pool to take advantage of an attractive view—or to avoid placing it in direct view of your neighbors' windows. Wind is another determining factor. If your yard is quite windy, locating the pool where your house, garage, privacy fence, or shrubs can serve as a windbreak will make swimming much more enjoyable, especially in mild weather.

Finally, pool location often depends somewhat on a home's room layout. Usually it's best to place the pool within a few steps of the kitchen or family room, particularly if you intend to use the pool area as an extension of your indoor living space.

When you have determined the pool's location, shape, and size, other elements of your plot plan will fall into place. These include the size and shape of the pool deck, the location of storage and pool equipment, the location of perimeter fencing and access points (gates), and any special features or amenities tagged as must-haves. Include on your plot plan any existing elements—such as trees, shrubs, outbuildings, power outlets, light fixtures, or hose bibs—that you intend to incorporate into the new scheme.

PROFESSIONAL POOL SOURCES

The following organizations may be able to help you locate reputable dealers and designers in your locale, assess the reliability of the pool products you're considering, provide you with background information on various aspects of pools and spas, and/or advise you on water quality issues.

National Spa & Pool Institute
2111 Eisenhower Ave.
Alexandria, VA 22314
www.nspi.org

National Swimming Pool Foundation
224 E. Cheyenne Mountain Blvd.
Colorado Springs, CO 80906

Independent Pool & Spa Service Association, Inc.
17715 Chatsworth St., Suite 203
Granada Hills, CA 91344

National Sanitation Foundation International
3475 Plymouth Rd.
Ann Arbor, MI 48105

United States Water Fitness Association, Inc.
P.O. Box 3279
Boynton Beach, FL 33424

International Association of Plumbing and Mechanical Officials
5001 E. Philadelphia St.
Ontario, CA 91761

Underwriters Laboratories
877/854-3597, or go to the website www.ul.com

NSF International
877/867-3435, or go to the website www.nsf.org

Pool Building Pointers

Before finalizing your plans, get familiar with the basics of building or installing a pool to avoid snags or delays once construction begins. The points on these pages apply to all pool projects; be aware that additional concerns pertaining to your pool type may arise as you plan.

Practical pool siting

First determine if you have sufficient access to your backyard for bringing in machinery and materials and, if necessary, hauling away excavated soil and anything else that needs to be removed to make way for your pool. Although most pool installations can be done with relatively small-scale equipment, such as a backhoe and an end loader, pool builders recommend an access corridor measuring at least 8 to 10 feet wide. In tight situations, builders can bring in a crane to lift large items, such as a one-piece pool shell, to your backyard from the front yard. Don't rent a crane for the duration of the project as that would add considerably to the total cost.

Another thing to determine quickly is whether your backyard provides a workable site for a pool. As noted earlier, a pool shell needs to be erected or placed on a level base so that its top edge is plumb all around. Pool decks must be nearly level, slanting slightly down on all sides so untreated water doesn't drain into the pool. Also, pool equipment must be located 25 to 50 feet from the pool and at the same elevation in order to perform properly. Finally, the pool site needs to be fairly close to an electrical outlet and a hose bib so that you can maintain the proper water level, hose off the deck regularly, and operate the equipment and underwater lighting.

Working with abovegrounds

All pools need a level, firm base to rest on, but this condition is especially critical for abovegrounds because their walls don't rely on backfilling, concrete decking, or bond beams for partial stiffening or support. When selecting the site for an aboveground unit, don't assume that soft fill dirt or sand can be added in spots to achieve a level grade; if necessary, plan to excavate deeper overall so that no fill is required. Soft fill may eventually shift beneath the pool liner, causing it to rupture. Also the excavation must be wide enough to provide good drainage around the bottom edge of the pool walls. Before filling the pool, make sure the top of the wall is perfectly level. If the pool is more than 1 inch off plumb from side to side, the water will be lopsided and will generate extra pressure against one side of the pool. This can cause the wall on that side to rupture. If you're installing a wood deck around the edge of the pool, it must be self-supporting; most aboveground pools aren't engineered to support a deck. If you plan to access your pool with a ladder, you need a nearby place to store it, because ladders for abovegrounds shouldn't be left in place when the pool isn't in use.

Working with ingrounds

If you're planning to excavate for an inground pool, one thing to check right away is the type of soil in your backyard. Certain soils or soil conditions can cause expensive delays during construction. Others can produce problems later, long after the work is done. Check the chart on page 43 to see what's involved with each soil type. If you're unsure what type best describes the soil in your backyard, have a local soils lab take core samples and analyze them for you.

Most inground pools are larger than abovegrounds, so you need to take some preliminary measurements to ensure your yard has enough buildable space for the pool you plan to install. Remember that the

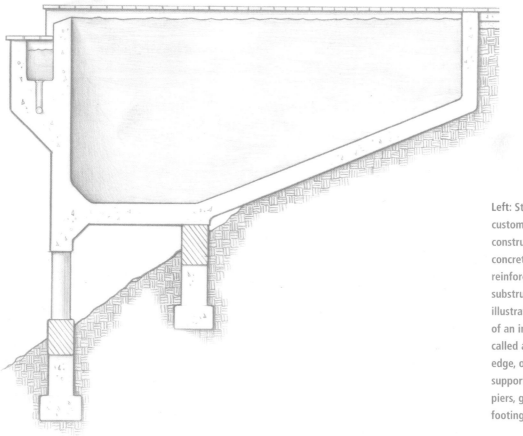

Left: Steep sites call for custom-engineered pools constructed of reinforced concrete, with steel or reinforced-concrete substructures. This illustration is an example of an infinity-edge (also called a disappearing edge, or horizon) pool supported by concrete piers, grade beams, and footings.

necessary to install a retaining wall to hold backfill in place in those areas and to provide a level grade for the pool deck. On sites where one side of the pool abuts an upward slope, either the grade must be cut back at least 6 feet at deck level and held with a retaining wall, or the pool itself must serve partially as a retaining wall. The latter is an option only for concrete pool shells, which can be designed and engineered for this purpose and custom-built on-site to conform to the grade. On slopes where the grade is steep, one side of the pool may be entirely exposed and the opposite side entirely embedded. In these cases, extra structural support is required to give the pool sufficient footing and to withstand the pressure of the hill. Also, take precautions to prevent surface rubble (rocks, gravel, or other debris) from rolling into the pool. On hillside sites like these, the cost of taming the grade can easily equal or exceed that of the pool itself, but the results are often spectacular.

Who Does What?

Unless you're versatile in a variety of construction trades, have plenty of time available, and can access the specialized equipment needed for building your pool project, you need to hire people with professional expertise and skills. As with other home improvements, there are several ways to go about this, and all involve signing on the dotted line at some point—that is, agreeing to purchase products and/or services for a specified sum subject to specified conditions.

Working with a dealer/installer

For modest-budget pool projects, you'll probably work with a dealer/installer. You visit a showroom and consult with a salesperson who helps you pick out a pool and pool accessories to best fit your wish list, budget, and site. Either the dealer's crew or an independent pool contractor hired by you or the dealer then installs the pool. Remember that even though dealer/installers are knowledgeable about pool shapes and finishes, with portfolios of completed projects for you to thumb through for ideas, their design expertise may be fairly limited. Also, be wary of dealerships that are simply sales operations that leave you to handle the installation phase. They are less likely to offer quality products and back them up with good customer service.

Working with a designer/builder

For complex or customized projects, the dealer/installer is only one option to consider. If you're intent upon giving your pool area a particular look or embellishing it with state-of-the-art features, you may want to consult a designer/builder or pool designer. Like architects or architectural designers, this professional offers design talent, new-product savvy, and technical know-how. Some also provide capable job supervision, serving as the project manager or general contractor. Elaborate, highly customized projects or those with special challenges may also require the services of other consultants—landscape architects, soils engineers, structural engineers, lighting designers, and spa dealer/builders.

All but the simplest pool projects involve hiring and supervising skilled and unskilled labor and using specialized tools and equipment. Here, a general contractor comes into play. The dealer/installer or designer/builder often performs this role. Or he or she may hire a general contractor for you (part of the service as project manager). If neither is the case, you'll need to find a contractor or do the job yourself. Pool contractors must be licensed by the state in which they work.

Rounding up the right team

To locate designers, builders, and dealers in your area, check the Yellow Pages of the phone book under "Swimming Pool Contractors, Dealers & Designers," "Swimming Pool Mfrs. & Distr.," or "Spas & Hot Tubs—Dealers." Other sources include websites of pool-industry organizations (see the listings on page 41) and recommendations from those in related fields, such as landscape design and residential architecture. Also, gather word-of-mouth recommendations from friends and neighbors who have pools.

Allow time to become familiar with a number of individuals or companies. Question each one about the quality of the

---

WHAT A CONTRACT SHOULD INCLUDE

Whether you use a contract supplied by your dealer or designer or have one drawn up by your lawyer, make sure it addresses all of the following points before you sign on the dotted line:

- The work that is to be done
- The work that is not to be done
- The equipment to be installed (list manufacturer and model number for each item)
- Itemized list of pre-pool costs (relocating utilities, regrading site)
- Itemized list of post-pool costs (landscaping, final grading, removal of debris)
- Payment schedule, including dates for sign-offs on approvals/inspections
- Compliance with zoning, codes, regulations, and covenants
- Releases of mechanic's liens each time payment is made
- Start and end dates
- Penalty clause for late completion
- Cancel clause, with penalty fee (if any) specified
- Date when owner assumes responsibility for pool maintenance
- Complete set of construction blueprints

Assuming there are no special problems to deal with regarding soil type, a standard contract probably would work for constructing a pool like this one. The shape is simple, the terrain is flat, and the finish materials are widely available.

products they carry, the warranties they offer on products and services, whether they have their own crew or work with subcontractors, how long they've been in business, and what trade or professional organizations they belong to. Also, ask for a list of at least five customer references, preferably homeowners whose pools are at least five years old.

Narrowing the field

Pare your list of candidates down to three or four, and then get estimates. When submitting your pool plan for estimates, make sure it's as detailed and specific as you can get at this point, and submit identical copies to all candidates to compare bids. Be wary of extremely high or low bids, and check estimates against each other to see if items are missing or new ones added to the plan you supplied. Missing items could be an indication of poor organization; additions may be included to point out some unwise shortcuts in your plan.

Meanwhile, take a closer look at the backgrounds of each of your candidates. Estimates may have similar bottom lines, so behind-the-scenes information will help you decide. Interview the homeowners listed as references, and visit those projects in person. Ask references if they would do a pool project with that individual or company again. Check the legal records on file at your county clerk's or recorder's office to see if any candidates have been sued recently.

Also, call the Better Business Bureau to find out if there are complaints on file against any candidates. Be wary if multiple suits or complaints show up against a given party.

Putting it down in black and white

Once you've chosen a pool contractor, it's time to draw up a contract. Most companies, particularly dealer/installers, provide a boilerplate contract, one that's been formulated for this type of construction, so you probably won't need a lawyer to draw one up from scratch unless you have an unusually elaborate pool in mind. However, do have your lawyer read the company's contract to make sure you're protected and all parts of the document will stand up in a court of law. No matter who provides the language, once the construction drawings (including all notes and specifications) are finalized, they become part of the contract and are legally binding documents.

Also, discuss and reach agreement regarding practical matters, whether specified in the contract or not. Will the crew need access to your bathroom? Will they respect your neighbors' property and privacy? Are there trees or plants to protect during the construction? (If so, note it on the construction drawings.) Will leftover material and construction debris be removed when the job is done? Does the contractor do the final grading, or is that your job?

Creating the Right Setting

Thoughtful planning and imaginative design can make a pool and its setting look as if they were made for each other.

As your pool plan takes shape, keep in mind that a great pool is much more than a place to take a dip. Properly planned, it can bring a whole new dimension of livability to your home—and give it a dramatic new look. Being near the water is often just as enjoyable as being in it, so a happy marriage between pool and setting will pay aesthetic dividends regardless of how much money you spend.

Finding the best scheme is partly a matter of sifting through a broad range of options. At first, the number of possibilities may seem bewildering, and for the most part there are no absolute right or wrong choices. But you can simplify the task by trusting your instincts and focusing on what feels right for you and your family. This chapter will give you a head start by highlighting some of the key design questions you're likely to confront along the way. The expertise of a professional designer can also make the planning process go more smoothly because designers already know most of the choices and have experience following their instincts in making these choices. However you approach this part of the plan, give your imagination free rein. Using your plot plan as a starting point, put your creative juices to work and assemble a poolside paradise by fleshing out the various parts of that basic framework in as much detail as possible.

The Basics of Good Design

Aside from basic guidelines for any situation involving aesthetic matters (see the box opposite), there are no inflexible rules for design. And although a well-padded budget allows more freedom and flexibility than a spare one, good design isn't reserved for large-budget pool projects. As you gather ideas, you may be tempted to adopt one approach as the absolute right choice. But keep in mind that every pool site—and the family that will use the pool—is unique; what's right for one isn't always right for another. So dive into the design process with an open mind and use your imagination.

Let it evolve

Coming up with your own best scheme is often a matter of trial and error, especially if you've had little or no experience planning pools or landscapes. Experimentation requires time and patience, one reason to let your pool area evolve over a period of several years and to use a master plan to guide its development. Also, some aspects of landscape design can be tricky for novices. A common mistake is to clutter available space with too many focal points, finish materials, or fussy details. Another pitfall is to misjudge the scale of key elements such as a shade structure, a waterfall, or a rock garden. For these major items, test your ideas with scale models or drawings. Trial-and-error construction is expensive and frustrating.

If you feel uncomfortable making subjective decisions or simply want to expedite the decisionmaking process without inviting disastrous results, the best course is to enlist the aid of a seasoned pool

Below: Layers of stone surrounding this pool combine with the dark bottom to create an exotic hideaway feel.

designer or landscape architect. Of course, these professionals charge a fee (either a flat fee or a percentage of the project's total cost), but they may save you money by steering you clear of wallet-draining options. This doesn't mean that an outsider makes all the choices; a real pro will work closely with you to create a design that feels right to both of you and that will mature gracefully as you complete each phase.

Proportionate to the site

Fitting an average-size swimming pool into a typical suburban backyard can be a challenge, particularly in neighborhoods where houses are close and yards are closed in with fences and mature vegetation. A 20×40-foot pool requires more than twice the square footage of a double garage—another large object in many backyards. It's important to choose a pool shape and size that leaves ample room for activity areas and breathing space around its perimeter.

If you want a 40-foot-long pool but think it would make your yard feel cramped, do a little creative thinking. Perhaps a simple principle of geometry will help: Within a given distance, diagonal lines are longer than straight ones. Angling your pool along a diagonal axis may yield the length you need without crowding your yard or encroaching on easements or setback lines.

Giving it a free-form shape that curves out of sight around a bend allows you to fit more pool into an irregular space.

If you simply want your pool to appear larger than its dimensions, consider tapering the sides of the pool slightly toward one end, thereby exaggerating normal perspective. Another option is to use only light-color finishes, which make objects look larger or farther away. A third choice is to carefully control the scale (size in relation to something else) of everything else nearby. This is a little trickier to accomplish on your own, but talk to your pool designer for suggestions. As always, let your instincts guide you: If it looks right and feels right, it probably is right.

BASIC DESIGN GUIDELINES

Creating an appropriate and functional setting for your pool is a matter of personal preferences, but there are a few basic guidelines to keep in mind to ensure the best results and to avoid disappointment—or costly revisions—once the project is finished. This chapter will touch on these points occasionally while exploring various options for developing a workable and appealing scheme.

- Major elements should be proportionate to one another and to the site.
- All the elements, large and small, should relate to one another and to the house as a whole.
- All the visual effects should complement one another rather than compete for attention or importance.
- All the parts should be compatible with activities or functions that will take place in the pool area.

One Level or Several?

Above: Rugged stone
walls and steps integrate
this rustic multilevel pool
with its hillside site. Tall
trees on the hill help
amplify the poolscape's
dramatic vertical thrust.

One question to ask yourself early in the design process is whether your pool setting will be mostly on one level or several levels. A closely related question is whether its overall look should be strongly horizontal or should incorporate a number of prominent vertical elements. A one-level scheme can be as appealing as a multilevel one, and both have advantages and trade-offs. Understanding how the two types of schemes differ and consciously opting for one or the other will help give your design a more purposeful continuity.

As expected, the terrain may be a major determining factor, particularly if it has a considerable slope. Carving out a level area large enough to put everything on one level may require some very costly cut-and-fill earthwork plus extensive retaining walls, and the result might look forced or brutal. On sites of this type, stairstepping the various elements of the pool area down the slope is a gentler, more naturalistic—and maybe more affordable—solution. An exception is a sloped site that levels out at the bottom. If you don't mind having your pool area isolated from, and several feet lower than, your house, a one-level scheme at the foot of the hill can be a dramatic and inexpensive way to set off a pool.

For yards with more typical terrain, the choice isn't so obvious. Where grade changes are moderate or negligible, one-level and multilevel schemes are equally feasible. There's usually room to install the pool itself on firm, well-settled soil, and it's fairly easy to add fill around the perimeter where necessary to extend the pool deck and make it large enough to accommodate all the activity areas. The only significant change of level might be from the pool area to the lawn.

It might, however, be more intriguing to accentuate or even amplify what little grade change there is by devising a multi-level scheme, with dining, lounging, and/or planting areas elevated a foot or two above the pool deck. Although probably more expensive than simply filling and leveling, multiple levels give the pool itself a subtle sense of enclosure and segregate wet areas from the rest of the poolscape. Also, where wind is a concern, raised areas surrounding a sunken pool can serve as built-in windbreaks.

Special considerations

Other factors may influence your choice, particularly where terrain isn't a strong

determinant. For instance, if your lot or the surrounding area provides a scenic or dramatic backdrop, you may want to keep your poolscape fairly simple so it complements the view rather than competes with it. If, on the other hand, you need to breathe new life into your backyard or camouflage an eyesore, you may want more than one level to build scenery and drama into the pool scheme itself. This poses yet another aesthetic challenge: how to strike an artful balance between your poolscape and the vertical elements that adjoin or surround it. Consciously integrating these two parts may not be easy, but when done well, the effect is often quite striking. The pools on these pages and the one on page 51 are good illustrations of this strategy.

You should avoid taking either type of approach to the extreme. A totally flat, featureless plane of concrete or stone can be rather uninviting, especially if it's some distance from the house and from trees or other sources of shade. And a profusion of level changes, executed with a complicated system of steps, planters, and retaining walls, can look cluttered and distracting, espe-

cially if the house is also a complex shape or has numerous exterior finish materials. Again, if you want to test your ideas but don't have a knack for translating them into three-dimensional sketches, build a rough model from clay or layers of cardboard. As your model takes shape, it will quickly become apparent if your scheme is too stark or too complicated. Of course, this is one of many aesthetic question marks that a professional designer is trained to help you grapple with, if you decide to go that route.

Above: Placing the spa and seating areas high above the pool adds to the grand feeling of this water space.

Below: Having the far side of this pool higher than the side closest to the house makes the yard look larger.

Curved or Linear?

About 60 years ago, when backyard pools were beginning to become affordable for mainstream Americans, homeowners had basically two choices: rectangular or kidney-shape. These are still classic shapes, but today's pool buyer can choose from virtually any shape imaginable. After flipping through countless showroom catalogs and clicking through the photogallery images on various pool manufacturers' websites, you may find yourself wondering how to zero in on the pool of your choice. One starting point is to decide whether you prefer a curved or a linear design. These two general types remain fairly distinct even after 60 years of product growth in the pool industry. If you have a definite preference for one or the other, you can handily rule out a large portion of the offerings.

Practical considerations

There are practical reasons for favoring one over the other, and you need to decide for yourself how much weight each deserves. For instance, linear pools are generally cheaper to build or install than curved ones. Curved surfaces are harder to fabricate; they require highly technical equipment and processes and/or highly skilled labor. Mass production has dramatically reduced the cost of a curved pool shape, but similar rectangular designs are still less expensive. Also, it's often more labor-intensive to fit paving materials around the edges of a curved pool, and it usually involves more waste. Some curved pools lack a straight run of open water long enough for lap swimming—unless you swim curved laps. They also, however, lack the sharp corners and crisp edges typical of linear pools—often concerns for safety-minded parents of young swimmers.

Your site conditions may also direct your range of choices somewhat but not as much as you might think. Many of today's manufactured pools are available in several sizes, so you're likely to find the size you need for any of the pool shapes that strike your fancy. And both linear and curved pools are available in thousands of different configurations, so you're bound to find several that fit the bill, no matter how irregular your pool's footprint needs to be.

Personal preferences

Although practical matters such as site and budget have to be factored in, selecting a pool is largely a matter of personal taste. Therefore, a bit of basic psychology comes into play. Curved lines tend to convey relaxation and hospitality, while straight lines tend to convey a reassuring sense of order and control. Both can be soothing, but for different reasons. Curved lines generally have more humanistic qualities, whereas straight lines tend to emphasize abstract concepts. If you find that a linear pool leaves you feeling cold, then you should follow your instinct and explore the options in curved pools. On the other hand, if you find the irregular, meandering outlines of a curved pool vaguely unsettling or lacking in focus, you should look seriously at the options in the linear category.

To some extent, personal preferences are influenced by cultural or historical associations. For example, people tend to associate

POOL & SPA POINTERS

If the pool that best fits your yard turns out to be smaller than you had imagined, remember this paradox of nature: A pool that is properly sized for its site will look larger than it really is whereas a pool that is too big for its site will appear smaller—and will seem awkwardly cramped too.

straight lines with classical design and, therefore, with formality, even though linear pool shapes can be just as irregular and asymmetrical as curved ones are. They also tend to associate straight lines with contemporary or modern architecture, despite the fact that some of the most notable examples (such as Frank Lloyd Wright's Guggenheim Museum in New York City) are strikingly curvilinear. Regional preferences are also an influence. Curved pools tend to be more common in warm, sunny climates, while linear pools tend to be more common in northern climates. If you live in a northern climate in a contemporary-style house, you may want to lean toward a more linear pool shape. If you live in a rambling, Mediterranean-style house in the Sunbelt, you may want to go with a softly curved free-form shape.

Formal or Informal?

Above: The rocky edges of
this pool give it an
informal feel. Combined
with the disappearing
edge broken punctuated
with one palm tree and a
single boulder, the pool
has the feeling of being
part of the rugged hillside
it sits.on.

Choosing between a formal and an informal pool-area design was once as simple as choosing a pool's shape: formal poolscapes were symmetrical; informal ones were asymmetrical, with a kidney shape. The rapid proliferation of pool shapes and finish materials in recent years and the accompanying trend toward ever-more-elaborate backyard poolscapes have provided many more design options to pick from and blurred the boundaries between formal and informal design.

In its purest form, formal design is characterized by simple geometric shapes arranged symmetrically and treated with subdued or neutral colors and subtle or no detailing. Informal design is characterized by irregular shapes, asymmetrical arrangements, robust colors, and rustic or exotic surface treatments. With either extreme, your pool could have straight lines and curves, as well as either a traditional or a contemporary flavor.

Cultural influences

Both types of pool designs have deep roots in the cultural past. Formal-style poolscapes, with their characteristic urns, fountains, classical columns, and symmetrical curves and arches, originated in ancient Rome, when wealthy families had homes with courtyard pools. Informal poolscapes, characterized by rough stone ledges, timber-frame gazebos, meandering pondlike pools, and rustic rock waterfalls, date back to the Romantic Age in England and Europe, when it became fashionable to glorify and mimic the natural beauty of rural landscapes.

Today, as people travel to exotic and romantic corners of the earth, either in person or via the media, they bring home additional ideas about how to design at-home vacation getaways. Two such imports are the Mediterranean and the Floridian styles. The Mediterranean is a semiformal look, with classical features and finishes but an asymmetrical layout. The Floridian is quite informal, with swirling, free-form pool and deck shapes and bold, tropical splashes of color. Both styles are particularly popular in coastal areas where people build retirement homes and adopt a leisure-oriented lifestyle.

One of the newest wrinkles in informal pool design is the total-illusion backyard getaway. Similar to the total-illusion effects created for Disney's theme parks, this approach to poolscaping goes far beyond the normal bounds of creating a pleasant setting for a pool. Some examples expand on the Floridian theme by creating a tropical-island look. Others take their cue from the Romantic Age by creating a rustic, woodsy look. The total-illusion approach has become so popular that pages 60–63 exlore it in detail.

Whether or not you want to create a total-illusion look, most people favor an informal or semiformal look of some sort. This is a good fit for today's casual lifestyle, especially in the suburbs and in leisure-oriented communities. Informal poolscapes are also a good fit for many of the homes in those communities—ranch-style ramblers, rustic farmhouses, and brick and stucco bungalows or cottages.

Still, the formal look is a favorite choice for those looking for an effective antidote against the strains and visual clutter of everyday life. The elegant simplicity and balance of formal design can make a pool a soothing oasis in the midst of an increasingly hectic, noisy, crowded world, and formal design adapts easily to small, closed-in yards that lack the space needed for a rambling layout. Also, the clean, simple lines of classic formalism tend to make small spaces feel larger. As cities become more urban and backyards begin to shrink, formal pool designs probably will gain in popularity.

Below: An intricate mosaic-tile scheme, handrails with curlicues, and two wraparound staircases add formality to this pool, as well as a generous touch of whimsy.

Right: Unifying design elements blend this pool/spa seamlessly with the house. One visual tie is the home's distinctive stucco wall treatment, which repeats as a design motif in the poolscape's planters and retaining walls.

Unified Elements

Opposite, below: This pool's perimeter jogs around low-slung planters, shallow steps, and a reef. The slim rectangular shapes, rendered in contrasting finishes, are stacked in layers, another unifying motif—one that is a natural extension of the home's ground-hugging profile.

Outfitting your yard with a well-equipped pool area involves filling it with a broad assortment of objects—some large, some small—that you obtain from various sources or order custom-made. Besides the pool itself, this list may include a pool deck, a storage or equipment shed, a fencing system, retaining walls and steps, some type of shade structure or privacy screen, an outdoor refreshment bar or grill area, and several pieces of outdoor furniture. A thoughtfully organized plot plan will give these objects a degree of order, but unless there is something else that ties them together and to your house visually, your pool area may take on a haphazard, disjointed look.

Well-designed poolscapes avoid the haphazard look by relying on what professional designers call a unifying aesthetic. In other words, all the parts of the design seem cut from the same cloth. They share the same palette of colors and textures, they have the same or similar shapes and details, and they express the same architectural style. Normally, a designer supplies this unifying aesthetic automatically by using artistic vision to fuse the various elements together and to select ready-made items

that fit or adapt easily to the vision. If, however, you are serving as your own designer, you'll need to supply this vision yourself and use it to filter out anything that doesn't fit.

Start with your house

Your home's architectural style should be the major ingredient and the starting point for this vision. Not only will your house be part of the setting for your pool, but your pool also will become an extension of your house. Therefore, take note of the features that define your home's character or style, such as its overall shape (two-story colonial, one-story ranch or bungalow, one-story cottage), its exterior surface treatments, its window and door styles, and any special elements that give it additional personality (brackets, raked eaves, stone chimneys, columns, arches). Use these notes as a guide when selecting shapes, finishes, and detailing for the various elements in your poolscape.

Another major ingredient of your vision is the shape you choose for your pool. As noted on pages 54–55, your home's architectural style should have a strong influence on this decision. If your home is formal, you should seriously consider a

formal or semiformal pool shape. If your home has a rustic or rambling character, you should seriously consider an informal shape.

One of the easiest ways to unify your home and pool area is to use the same or complementary finish materials on both. Repeating the house siding and trim on the poolside storage shed or cabana will make the smaller structure look as if it belongs. Repeating the stone veneer of the home's chimney or entry columns as a border around the pool deck will counteract the newness of the pool paving and provide a subtle sense of unity and history. Other links with the house can be expressed by repeating roof lines, sash details, door hardware, lighting fixtures, and gable vents.

Link up with the landscaping

Landscape design can also be a strong unifying device. If your home already seems comfortably mated with its site, take note of the landscape elements that have been used to achieve this effect, such as terraces, decks, planters, paths, garden walls, fences, hedges, and foundation plantings. Then decide which of these elements can be extended, repeated, or simulated when you add your poolscaping. In some cases, practical considerations will rule out exact duplication of a given shape or material. For example, the flagstone on your garden paths may no longer be available or may be too expensive for paving an area as large as a pool deck; but if you allow time to do a little searching and are willing to invest in more than mere expedience, you may find a paving block or a stamped-concrete finish that harmonizes nicely with the stone. Likewise, the charming brick parapets that anchor your rear terrace may be too expensive to duplicate as 6-foot-high walls around the pool perimeter, but they might translate very nicely as square brick accent piers for a less-expensive fencing system.

Unify with motifs

An even more subtle means of tying everything together visually is to incorporate a series of design motifs. Like themes or melodies in musical compositions, motifs are the artistic glue that unifies various objects or surfaces by repeating at certain intervals, either exactly or in interesting variations. Examples include distinctive edge and corner treatments, grid patterns, shapes borrowed from nature (and usually stylized to give them an artful spin), and shapes or patterns that echo a family's special interests (such as boating, woodworking, crafts, or collecting).

Above: This spa is a good example of how motifs can become variations on a theme. Some of its rounded corners are covered in white stucco; others are wrapped with tiny blue mosaic tiles. The round-edge motif repeats in larger format, and with another material, along the lip of the terra-cotta tile deck.

Rustic Hideaways

Since the 1950s, the typical suburban house—and backyard—has gotten considerably larger. Also, as noted in the first chapter, families are spending more leisure time at home and doing more entertaining there. Together, these trends have triggered a rapid growth in the number of backyard pools and in a whole new dimension of informal-style poolscaping that aims at creating total-illusion backyard getaways. Although this approach to pool design requires major investments of money, technical expertise, and design talent and usually monopolizes a yard, it is steadily winning converts coast to coast.

One popular version of this new total-illusion approach is the rustic retreat. Rustic retreats are designed to look like real-life ponds, river basins, small lakes, or hidden lagoons, complete with waterfalls, rock outcroppings, lush foliage, and maybe even beaches or brooks. The aim is to make the pool appear as though it occurred naturally and to create a little piece of paradise—a place to escape the hard-edged or predictably ordered landscapes of urban life.

Rustic design varies widely depending on the homeowners' budget, the amount of space available, and the region. Pools of this type, however, have certain common features. In addition to an irregular or free-form pool shape—an element typical of most informal designs—the rustic pool usually features an edging of rugged, casually arranged real or synthetic stone and boulders, as well as plantings that overhang the edging in spots. On compact sites, a rustic scheme may also include a lush wall of greenery to maintain an illusion of total escape to another world. Where space is ample, the pool may be the focal point of a woodland clearing or meadow. Whatever the theme or setting, the landscaping for a rustic scheme tends to be a big-ticket item on the budget—at least 25 percent of a pool area's total cost. Lighting is generally concealed or camouflaged, and some may be

designed to resemble moonlight. Also, the pool itself is usually given a dark finish, much like the dark-colored bottoms of natural ponds or lakes, so that the color of the water also looks natural.

New materials

A broad range of new materials that make it easy to duplicate nature's rustic hues and textures is boosting the popularity of this trend. Real stone and the labor to install it can be quite pricey, so pool builders and designers have turned to an expanding palette of new synthetic products that look like stone but cost about $7 to $8 per square foot less. Some, but not all, are easier and/or

This rustic pool/spa seems to be the work of Mother Nature. Naturalistic touches include dark-tone water, an irregular-shape flagstone deck, several small waterfalls, real rock outcroppings, and a thick wall of lush greenery.

less expensive than stone to install. Two examples are stained and stamped concrete, both of which are paving surfaces installed in large sections like conventional concrete, but they can be made to resemble slabs of stone or a solidified sediment deposit. Stamped concrete also can mimic river rock, pebbles, cobbles, and other natural paving materials. Other examples blend pulverized rubble with cement or polymers and are then molded into various stone look-alikes and used as veneers, pavers, capstones, and ledges or as full-round rocks and boulders for waterfalls and edgings. (For additional information on these and other pool-area finish materials, turn to pages 64–65.)

RUSTIC RETREATS
Design Characteristics
- Free-form pool shape
- Jagged, stone-edged pool
- Overhanging pool plantings
- Rough-textured stone decking
- Dark-tone pool water
- Boulder-strewn waterfall
- Wall of greenery
- Tall grasses and water plants
- Hidden lighting

Evoking the Islands

While some total-illusion pool schemes resemble woodland retreats, others re-create the exotic allure of a tropical island. Like the rustic versions, island-theme designs usually feature an irregular or free-form pool, lush plantings, large rocks or ledges, and at least one waterfall. Several significant differences, however, set tropical-island designs apart from their rustic counterparts.

First, an island-theme pool area may or may not be totally naturalistic. Some examples resemble a naturally created island beach or lagoon, whereas others appear to be patterned after the elaborate poolscapes of tropical vacation resorts. Another difference is the overall palette. Tropical designs rely more on light-color finishes and bright accents. Paved areas are usually off-white or sand-tone to mimic a pristine island beach or an elegantly appointed resort-hotel pool deck. The water is lighter and brighter too. Instead of the opaque, dark-tone water of a rustic-retreat design, the water in a tropical-theme pool evokes the transparent, sparkling blue or green hues of equatorial seas and resort pools. Finish materials and accent colors echo the vivid hues of tropical flowers and island architecture or the cool pastels of sea-misted sunrises and sunsets.

Landscape materials are another point of departure. In place of the conifers and deciduous trees of the rustic-theme designs, island-theme landscapes feature palms, bamboos, bird-of-paradise, and other exotic plants. And instead of limestone ledges or glacier-carved granite outcroppings, there may be lava-rock boulders or coral reefs.

Characteristic set pieces also help define the tropical scheme. Examples include a swim-up bar (an idea borrowed from designers of resort-hotel pools); thatch-roof shade structures or umbrellas (amenities that originated in the South Seas and along the Mexican Riviera); and louvered sunscreens, Georgian columns, and large wooden paddle fans (imports from British Colonial outposts in the Caribbean and the East Indies). Small details play a role, as well, usually in the

Below: This island-theme pool area resembles a tropical beachfront resort, complete with swim-up bar. Pebbly white aggregate paving on the pool deck mimics a white sand beach. The palm thatching on the bar's roof echoes the native huts of South Seas islanders. Palms and exotic under-plantings round out the illusion.

TROPICAL ISLAND RETREATS
Design Characteristics
- Free-form pool shape
- Exotic plantings
- Clear blue or green pool water
- Bright accent colors
- Off-white or sand-color pool deck

Left: Earthy stones gradually give way to deepening layers of blue, the same way the colors do along a shoreline.

Below: The spa nestles in its own grove of palms, offering a little oasis-within-an-oasis. The ceramic tile on its inner surface calls to mind the shimmering blue horizons of a tropical sea. Overflow from the spa forms a waterfall that cascades from the tawny stone wall into the pool.

form of nautical motifs such as shells, sea turtles, and starfish.

Regional connections

If a total-illusion setting is what you envision for your pool area, keep in mind that such schemes tend to be region-specific and can look artificial and forced if transplanted to a different locale or climate. Tropical-theme poolscapes that look perfectly appropriate in Sunbelt areas such as Florida or Southern California may seem totally out of place in northern regions where nothing tropical grows naturally. Similarly, rustic-woods poolscapes can seem awkwardly out of place in the desert Southwest, where hot sun and parched, treeless terrain rule out lushly forested wetlands. The illusion of a backyard getaway will be more convincing, rather than less, if its design relates somewhat to the real environment that lies just over the fence.

A Fitting Blend of Finishes

Above: Simple concrete with curved outside edges and an inside border of terra-cotta color tiles inexpensively dresses up this pool. Those choices left money in the budget for an elegant waterfall and built-in spa.

As with other home improvements, many of the key decisions for your pool project involve finish materials. In addition to the finish for the pool shell itself, you need to select horizontal surfaces such as the pool deck, walkways, and stair treads; vertical surfaces such as retaining walls and stair risers; exterior finishes for outbuildings such as a storage shed or gazebo; fencing, handrails, and privacy screens; and outdoor furniture. Each category has a broad range of options, so you may want a professional designer to help you zero in on the ones that will work best. Good designers can save time and trouble because they're experienced at putting together just the right mix of colors, textures, and accents.

POOL & SPA POINTERS

Scale is very important when planning features such as waterfalls, spas, shade structures, privacy screens, or even the deck. A waterfall that **upstages the pool area with massive boulders or ledges can make a modest pool look like a puddle. Cover a deck with closely spaced pavers rather than oversize tiles to make the pool itself seem larger by contrast.**

Aesthetic considerations

Selecting finishes poses the same kind of aesthetic challenge you'd face if you were redecorating or building a home: how to make it all look coordinated and harmonious. It's important, therefore, to establish a basic palette to guide your selections. Start with one or two materials, finishes, or colors that you favor and that work well with your home's exterior; then begin collecting samples and assembling them in a scrapbook format you can carry with you and refer to as you shop for additional materials and products or confer with your designer. As you flip through showroom catalogs or click through the product information windows on websites, watch for subtle variations or alternatives for each type of item. In addition to color choices, check whether it comes in patterns as well as solids, a matte finish as well as gloss or satin, textures as well as smooth surfaces. Keep in mind where each material will be used. A finish too slippery for the pool deck might be perfect for countertops in the grill area, and a textured tile with detailing too subtle to be noticed in the bright sun of the pool deck might work nicely as a border in the gazebo floor. As you gather samples, take them home and test them together outdoors in situations similar to those where they would be used as part of the pool scheme.

Practical considerations

One of the most important considerations is cost. Finish materials comprise a big chunk of the budget, so think about where to economize and where to splurge. This is one area in which a master plan can guide your decisionmaking. For example, a major up-front cost would be the paving and coping for the pool deck, but you could rough in the walkways with pea gravel temporarily until your budget allows for brick or flagstone.

Another practical concern is durability. Materials that will hold their finish for a

long time and remain structurally sound are a good value. Under a pool's harsh conditions, inferior materials quickly fade, crack, corrode, or crumble and may require costly replacement before your budget rebounds from the initial construction cost. Generally, more durable products are more expensive to purchase and install. Cost alone isn't an assurance of high quality; without careful evaluations, you could pay for snob appeal, not for longer-term durability.

A third practical concern is maintenance. Most of the materials you select will be exposed all year long to various weather conditions; some will also sustain heavy use during the pool season; and all will accumulate dirt, dust, bugs, stains, leaves, needles, seedpods, grass clippings, and other debris. Plain, light-color products show dirt and stains easily, while patterned, dark-color ones tend to hide them. Porous materials absorb dirt and stains; high-gloss materials shrug them off. Also, materials with fewer seams or grout lines tend to be easier to clean because they have fewer spots where dirt and stains can gain a foothold.

Two other considerations to keep in mind are safety and comfort. Some easy-to-clean materials, such as glazed ceramic tile and polished marble, have slick surfaces that pose safety hazards for wet feet or produce dangerous or annoying glare in bright sunlight. Also, some surfaces absorb heat readily, causing discomfort for bare skin. Examples include metal handrails, dark slate pavers, and dark-painted wood decking.

Understanding Finishes

As you compare materials, you'll begin to understand the advantages and drawbacks of each option. Some options, however, offer superior performance and/or design flexibility in a given price category, so a little savvy shopping can pay big benefits in the long run.

Budget-friendly options

The chart on the facing page will help you get started. If you're working within a fairly strict budget and if your pool scheme doesn't pose any special construction challenges or involve any highly complex design elements, basic options like those listed in the chart may be good choices. For example, poured concrete provides long-term usability and optimum design flexibility at a modest cost per square foot. It can be used for virtually any paving application; it can be stained, tinted, scored, or stamped to give it extra eye appeal; and it can be troweled satiny-smooth, given a finish coat of fine plaster (as in concrete pool shells), or washed down to a pebbly exposed-aggregate finish as it sets up. Keep in mind, however, that all concrete pours eventually develop cracks, no matter how well reinforced. Some cracks start and remain minor; others cause serious damage and require major repair. Also, laying concrete is usually a job best done by skilled laborers, not do-it-yourselfers. And concrete tints and stains often fade after several years' exposure to sun, seasonal shifts, and heavy traffic.

Pavers are another good workhorse option. Like concrete, pavers offer design flexibility and long-term durability at a low cost. They also provide good traction for wet feet because their surfaces are porous rather than highly polished. Common varieties are bricks, squares, cobbles, and interlocking pavers. Pavers are less prone to cracking than large expanses of concrete because the pieces are smaller to begin with. Another advantage is that they can be installed without hiring skilled labor because they're usually laid dry (without mortar or grout) on a bed of compacted sand. A disadvantage is the many narrow joints, which tend to collect dirt and debris and become breeding grounds for weeds.

Luxury options

If your budget is ample, you may instead want to consider a stone or tile finish for your paved areas. Although the material itself often is two or three times more costly than poured concrete and involves expensive, time-intensive skilled labor to install, you'll enjoy many years of low-maintenance durability and lasting good looks. Drawbacks vary depending on the specific material and use in question. For instance, highly polished stone can produce dangerous glare and doesn't provide good traction. On the positive side, it is relatively easy to keep clean. Thin slabs of stone tend to crack (even when laid on a base of thick mortar), and dark stone can get uncomfortably hot when exposed to direct sun for long periods. Similar cautions apply to ceramic tile. For either material, be sure to use honed, matte, or textured varieties on horizontal surfaces such as walkways, stair treads, or the pool deck. For vertical surfaces, especially under or just above the waterline in a pool or spa, use glazed or polished varieties.

High-tech finishes

Technological breakthroughs in recent years have greatly expanded the palette of finish materials now available in the marketplace. Some are brand-new products; others are major upgrades. Some have been developed specifically as finishes for pool shells and pool decks; others have been developed for more general use as cladding materials, wood substitutes, and fencing components, applications that come into play in the areas surrounding a pool. Most tend to be moderately more expensive than their traditional counterparts but offer superior durability and/or design possibilities.

Finish coatings for pool shells is one product area that has undergone dramatic changes. Once dominated by a single product type—white plaster—it now includes fancy, highly colorful aggregate coatings made with quartz granules, multicolored pebbles, and polymer bonding agents; special high-performance plaster compounds

Characteristics of Finish Materials

MATERIAL	DURABILITY	COLOR CHOICES	BASE REQUIRED	EASE OF INSTALLATION	COST— MATERIAL ONLY
Brick	Good	Organic reds, tans, browns, grays	Dry-fit over gravel and sand base, or mortared over concrete	Dry-fit is relatively easy; mortared requires skill	$3–$4 per square foot
Flagstone	Good	Reds, cream, yellows, grays, dark blues, browns, some variations	Dry-fit over gravel and sand base, or mortared over concrete	Dry-fit is relatively easy; mortared requires skill	$3–$4 per square foot
Quarry tile	Excellent	Organic reds, tans, browns, grays	Mortared and grouted over concrete	Requires skill	$1–$2 per square foot
Concrete slab	Excellent	Dull gray; can be colored	Dry-fit over gravel and sand base	Simple but labor intensive	About $1 per square foot
Concrete paver	Excellent	Organic reds, tans, browns, grays	Dry-fit over gravel and sand base, or mortared over concrete	Dry-fit is relatively easy; mortared requires skill	$2–$3 per square foot
Unglazed ceramic tile	Excellent	Unlimited	Mortared and grouted over concrete	Requires skill	$3–$25 per square foot

made with finely ground marble dust and special hardeners and binders; superslick, fungus-proof fiberglass; and plaster mixed with colored glass beads. Although these coatings may cost twice as much as ordinary white plaster, their bright hues and patterns hide the mottling and staining that eventually occurs when plaster is exposed to pool chemicals and water.

Synthetic stone cladding and paving products represent another big area of innovation. As noted in the discussion of rustic-retreat pool schemes on pages 60–61, many of these new stone look-alikes are very convincing. One type, called cast stone, is made with pulverized quarry waste, cement, and special binders or strengtheners and poured into molds to form veneer-stone pieces that fit together and wrap around corners. One advantage of cast stone is that it costs about 25 percent less than real stone, and is usually more widely available.

Other new materials and finishes are available for outdoor structures, outdoor furniture, and fencing. Steel and natural or treated wood, the traditional options for such features, are gradually yielding ground to high-tech alternatives such as plastic-impregnated wood, PVC vinyl extrusions, cast aluminum, and fiberglass. One advan-

tage these products have over their traditional counterparts is long-term resistance to moisture damage—a distinct plus for any material used near a pool. Plastic wood, also called composite wood, is a blend of real wood and high-grade plastic (polymers). It can be sawed, nailed, and screwed like real wood yet never needs painting or staining. At $8.50 per square foot, it costs about 40 percent more than treated wood ($6.00 per square foot), but you can recoup the extra expense in about five years through savings on maintenance. Plastic wood is also cooler to walk on than painted wood. PVC vinyl has already made inroads in the fencing and shade structure market. Vinyl fence and lattice products are very realistic-looking and, like plastic wood, never need painting or staining. Again, you pay extra for vinyl's zero-maintenance durability, but it still costs less than top-grade wood fencing such as knot-free cedar or redwood. Fiberglass, a material used for several decades to build boat hulls and pool shells, is now used for lightweight mesh security fencing and cool-to-the-touch handrails. Besides being easy to lift and friendly to bare skin, fiberglass is a solid-color material like vinyl and it never needs painting or staining.

Smart Landscaping

An attractive setting or backdrop is one ingredient of good poolscaping. Another is a blend of creature comforts and low maintenance. And a third is compatibility with your budget and your long-range plan. A thoughtful design can achieve all these aims at once, but it won't happen by accident, so address these concerns early on and—if necessary—get some input from a design professional before moving ahead.

Right: Incorporating plants softens even the hardest edges. These small cutouts in the deck accommodate the refreshing element of flowers and greenery.

Easy on the eyes

Your pool will become the centerpiece of your backyard as well as a point from which to view other areas of interest, ones within or beyond your yard's boundaries. A well-developed landscape plan preserves and enhances good views and blocks or minimizes undesirable views. Begin the planning process by identifying the view corridors on your plot plan. This allows you to see your yard from different vantage points, including some you may not have considered

Below: By folding the landscaping elements around this pool, it almost becomes a pond.

before. For instance, stand where your plan indicates the main lounging area will be and look around. If the view isn't particularly pleasant—or if you find yourself looking directly at a neighbor's windows— landscaping may be able to correct the problem. If the view is especially nice, landscaping can accentuate it.

Landscaping can also help merge the pool with the site and house. Extending the pool deck into the yard and/or close to the house is one way to tie everything together. Another is to weave part of your home's landscaping into the poolscape by expanding walkways, foundation plantings, raised planters, trellises, hedges, and lawn areas. Or, use the house, the existing landscape, and the new landscape to create a subtle

sense of enclosure for the pool area, making them all work together as parts of an outdoor room. Fences, retaining walls, tiered layers of shrubs or shade trees, and rows of flowering bushes define the outer boundaries of the room, while smaller-scale plantings and special features (such as a waterfall or fountain) furnish it.

Easy to live with

When selecting plant species for your landscape scheme and deciding where to put them, appearance is only one of several factors that should influence your decisions. Some trees, for example, are particularly messy and can cause extra maintenance work—both within the pool and on the pool deck. To some extent, you can avoid extra work by planting larger trees well away from the pool and isolating them with a buffer zone of shrubs, planters, or lawn. Deciduous trees such as walnuts, sycamores,

and soft maples are among the worst offenders, but long-needled conifers can also be a nuisance. All trees generate a certain amount of fallout, but if you want to plant one near the pool for shade or artistic effect, look for an ornamental species or one that has small-scale foliage and no seedpods or fruits.

Functional Structures

lthough not an absolute necessity, outbuildings can add substantially to the enjoyment of a pool area. Besides providing convenient and valuable storage space for pool equipment, chemicals, pool-cleaning tools and supplies, outdoor furniture, and all the paraphernalia connected with water activities, thoughtfully designed outbuildings perform several other useful functions.

One of the most common uses for an outdoor structure near the pool is to provide shade for lounging, dining, or supervising. This can be achieved many ways: Attach a trellis or a strategically placed lattice screen to a storage shed, build a freestanding pergola along one side of the pool deck, or build a gazebo that perches near the deck or

nestles in the landscaping. If the storage shed is in a handy location for changing, it's a simple matter to expand it slightly to accommodate a separate compartment for this purpose. A space about the size of a half bath or powder room is adequate, equipped with a built-in bench, some wall hooks, and a waterproof flooring surface. Incorporate a small refreshment bar and work space near the lounging area if you plan to spend time with the whole family or entertain by the pool. The extra expense these conveniences entails is nominal compared to the total cost of a pool project, and it pays big dividends in the long run, not the least of which is less wear and tear on your indoor bathroom, kitchen, dining, and traffic areas. Also, creating a protected area outdoors makes it more practical to establish a permanent telephone location there, a feature that could prove invaluable in case of an emergency.

Consider the other benefits of including an outbuilding: For example, if one side of your pool will be in full view of the neighbors' yard or exposed to chilly winds at certain times of the day or year, why not use an outbuilding as a privacy screen or a windbreak—or both? Even if parts of the structure consist of see-through elements such as lattice, louvers, or closely spaced spindles, they may still provide a satisfying

Below left: This charming poolside structure performs multiple roles: storage for pool equipment, a changing room with a half bath, and a screen blocking the pool area from a side street.

Below right: The gazebo's front porch doubles as an outdoor shower.

Left: Perched a few feet above the pool deck, this gazebo dining area offers a handy spot to relax between dips and provides a comfortable place with an unobstructed view for grownups to supervise youngsters in the pool. For sites that lack mature trees, a gazebo also provides instant shade.

degree of enclosure and protection.

In addition to their many practical uses, outbuildings and other outdoor structures make handsome complements or focal points for landscapes. Arbors, fences, gazebos, garden sheds, grill areas, cabanas, and screened enclosures lend architectural weight and vertical counterpoint to any garden setting. They're especially effective in relatively flat yards or those that haven't yet acquired mature plant stock.

Costs for outdoor structures can range from a few hundred dollars for a pergola or a storage shed to several thousand dollars for a custom-designed poolhouse complete with outdoor kitchen, cable TV, shower, and changing room. Although the more elaborate versions are often constructed like conventional houses, with a concrete foundation, stud-framed walls, insulation, and drywall or paneled interiors, a simpler, more rustic approach can be just as attractive and usually makes more sense. If you are handy with tools, you can probably build your own outdoor structures by assembling a mail-order kit, ordering a set of project plans from a magazine, or creating your own design from scratch.

Artful Lighting

Above: Underwater and landscape lighting make this pool relaxing and enjoyable every hour of the day.

Extra livability and enjoyment are just two of the benefits of including a lighting system. With the flick of a switch or setting of an automatic timer, you can add several hours of poolside relaxation every day. A broad range of low-cost outdoor lighting products are widely available, and many can be installed quickly and easily by do-it-yourselfers.

The light stuff

The gear needed for a basic, multifaceted lighting plan can be purchased for about $1,500. It should incorporate five different aspects of your pool layout: the pool itself (especially underwater lighting); traffic areas, such as walkways, steps, gates, paths, and the pool deck; activity areas, such as an outdoor kitchen; background elements, such as landscaping; and special features, such as a waterfall or bridge. The lighting gear and the quality of light varies depending on which part of the pool area is involved. For example, underwater lighting should have at least two different brightness settings: a low setting when the pool isn't in use and higher settings when it is. Another option is special color effects in underwater lighting. Lighting for pathways and other traffic areas should be low-key, indirect, and white or bug-repellent yellow. Most outdoor lighting is placed so that the light source isn't directly visible to prevent glare and momentary blindness, a common occurrence at night outdoors. Lighting in activity areas may be in more conventional locations, such as directly overhead on beams or rafters, because such areas are usually roomlike spaces with perimeter surfaces to contain and reflect the light, creating an ambient glow that heads off glare and keeps the darkness at bay.

Decorative lighting effects

Indirect lighting, the type needed for most areas outdoors, is most appealing if done with a blend of several different techniques. One, called downlighting, involves directing the light straight down and illuminating primarily with the light that

Ground lighting

bounces back upward. Spotlights and garden-path lights are usually used as down-lights to create a nonglaring pool of light in a specific spot, such as a crosswalk or stair landing. Uplighting throws a beam of light upward from a concealed source to illumi-nate a vertical surface or object, such as a tree or a garden wall. Grazing casts light downward or upward almost parallel with a vertical surface, creating shadow patterns to accentuate surface textures. Backlighting involves directing light toward objects behind the one you want to accentuate, defining its shape partly by silhouette and partly by a halo of softly bounced light. Shadowing involves using a single light source to throw interesting shadows against an otherwise plain surface.

Try before you buy

To give your lighting scheme maximum eye appeal, do some experimenting before you buy and install your system. Using a few outdoor power cords and some temporary light sources (metal-shaded trouble lights work well), test various lighting techniques in your pool area after the sun goes down to see which effects work best and how many light sources are needed. (Note: Outdoor power extension cords should not be used as permanent components of the installed

Underwater lighting

system and not at all for underwater light-ing.) Avoid using too many sources; it's easy to get carried away and end up with dis-tracting or cluttered lighting. And avoid repeating the same effect too often; alternate two or three different effects so that the light sources vary as they do in nature. For example, instead of lighting an entire walk-way with a long, repetitive sequence of lights, alternate frequently with backlight-ing or grazing. Later, do a little more experimenting by roughing in the system and fine-tuning it, making minor adjustments in placement, light levels, and light angles before doing your permanent installation.

Below: By using a variety of lighting sources, this pool is nicely accented and doesn't detract from the striking skyline view.

Wall lighting

Clean Lines, Gentle Angles

For a better idea of how the various guidelines discussed in this chapter can help you create the right setting for your pool, take a close look at the three real-life examples shown here and on the following pages. Each has a different personality and addresses a different set of site requirements, and all three offer useful lessons that you can put to work in your own backyard.

The first example is a lean, sophisticated poolscape that uses gentle angles and subtle textures and hues to create visual impact within the tight confines of an urban backyard. The poolscape is mostly a one-level scheme, with the spa raised slightly on a small wood deck. One end of the pool angles toward the carport, which does double duty as a strong vertical counterpoint and privacy wall. Working with clean, uncluttered planes like these—vertically as well as horizontally—makes a small-site pool area feel serenely spacious. It's also a good way to stay on track with your budget; simple, flat, rectangular surfaces are usually the least expensive to construct and finish. Two other major yet subtle space-stretching ploys are at work in this design. One is the angled pool shape: Angling a pool along a diagonal axis allows you to fit more pool into a tight space without making it look crowded. Besides playing the angles, the designer of this pool also used color as a visual space stretcher. Most of the finish materials are soft shades of gray or gray-blue—the colors associated with distant horizons.

Although the design of this pool area is informal in terms of layout (asymmetrical in plan and pool shape), the effect is semiformal because of the subdued palette and elegantly spare detailing. Note how the linear character of each component is a unifying element to tie everything together. Rectangular shapes in the stone veneers repeat in the pool coping and tile borders, in the scored concrete pool deck, and in the wall planes and the beams of the carport. This low-key formalism can be effective for any type of pool site but is particularly fitting for small urban backyards because it offers a welcome respite from the visual clutter of the city.

Below: A pair of masonry walls clad in Pennsylvania bluestone serves as privacy screens between this urban pool area and a back alley. Rectangular shapes in the stones repeat in the Italian glass mosaic tiles that form a border above the waterline in the pool. One end of the pool angles gently, gaining a few extra feet lengthwise and defining the outdoor dining area.

Left: This hot tub perches on a low wood deck that adjoins the rear of the house. Angles in the deck steps echo those in the stone border of the pool deck and in the ends of the rafters that span the carport.

Below: Slabs of tinted concrete form a floating bench and a cap for the carport wall. The bench provides a place for swimmers to towel off before taking a seat in the dining area.

POOL & SPA POINTERS

Good landscaping can add livability to your pool area by tempering its climate. Strategically placed walls and trees can block chilly winds or create pockets of cool shade, extending the number of days that you can use the pool each year.

The second real-life example involves another typical backyard situation: a squarish, flat, expansive suburban site with bare open space and no strong visual boundaries along the perimeter. In many ways, it's the antithesis of the urban backyard, where cramped quarters call for visual tricks to create the illusion of space. Here, the challenge is to create a sense of place or enclosure without destroying the yard's pleasantly open feel.

The solution in this particular instance is a modified version referred to as a rustic retreat (see pages 60–61). Instead of a conventional pool design bordered by a paved pool deck and surrounded by a manicured lawn, this pool resembles a pond in the midst of a spacious meadow. Although not quite a total-illusion poolscape, it fulfills that concept in a number of ways. Its shape meanders informally, its edges are rimmed with rough stones and overhanging plants, and its water has the muted-green, semitransparent look of pond water.

Using a modified rustic-retreat approach on sites like this one makes sense for a number of reasons. The informal, rural character of a pond-style pool looks very much at home in suburban settings and with many types of suburban home styles, including ranches and farmhouses. Also, its rustic textures and casual, irregular outlines create a sense of place out in the middle of a large open, loosely defined area—just as a real pond provides a strong focus or arrival point for an open meadow. In addition, the casual curves and meanderings of a pond-style design provide welcome relief from the severely straight boundary lines typical of suburban lots. Other design elements reinforce this happy interrelationship between poolscape and site. Large boulders placed along the shoreline of the pool lend natural

Below: This naturalistic pool/spa curves out of sight around a bend just as a real pond would. Most of its shoreline is defined by beds of grasses, heathers, and low shrubs and by a slim border of rough stone, not by a conventional pool deck.

character to the landscaping and also relieve the site's uniform flatness. Similar effects could be achieved with clumps of tall grasses. Near the spa, a pyramidal juniper provides a focal point for the entire layout. Again, you can achieve a similar effect with a tall weeping willow or a trio of paper-bark birches.

Pond-in-the-meadow schemes offer practical advantages as well as aesthetic ones. In nature, ponds tend to have few or no trees along the shoreline. The plant life that does thrive there is mostly reeds, grasses, and small-scale bushes. Therefore, it's fairly easy to create a realistic, low-maintenance pondscape. Large trees—and the mess they generate at certain times of the year—can be confined to the perimeters of your yard, and so can fancy flowering shrubs and perennials—the kinds that draw pesky insects. If you want to manufacture some shade near the pond's edge, you can do this with a small tree, a gazebo, or a pergola, any of which will blend in nicely with the natural, rural feel of the place.

Above: Like the pool, the spa has an irregular shape bordered by rough stone blocks. Wavy rows of cobbles wrap around the spa area to form a terrace for dining and lounging.

Left: Steps leading into the pool from the dining terrace and spa double as reefs for relaxing in the water between swims. A squared-off block of stone forms part of the coping near the spa; it provides a spot to perch and dip your toes in the water.

Tucked Into the Woods

This real-life pool setting deals with a site situation different from the others and is somewhat less typical, but nevertheless familiar. Instead of a tight urban lot or a flat, empty, rectangular one, it's a hilly, wooded, picturesque yard overlooking a lake. Adding an attractive, multifunctional pool area to a setting that has so much going for it may sound easy, but in some ways, it is more of a challenge. How do you improve on something already picture-perfect? How do you accommodate an active family without making the setting look invaded? And how do you turn the terrain into an advantage rather than a drawback?

The answer was to design the pool area as a total-illusion rustic retreat. Giving the pool a meandering, organic shape and rimming it with rugged stone walls and a stone-paved deck make it look as though it has always been there. To enhance the illusion and to take advantage of the hilly terrain, a large waterfall was added near the base of a hill. Other major features, such as the spa and a dining terrace, cluster around the pool at various levels, following the site's natural changes in elevation. Near the waterfall, a multipurpose pool house nestles against the hillside, providing changing rooms, a lounging area, and convenient clutter control for pool equipment and water sports gear. The boulders and stone blocks have been carefully selected to match native stones on the property so the poolscape appears to merge seamlessly with its surroundings. The wooded hills serve as a natural enclosure, completing the effect of a total world-unto-itself hideaway.

Below: Nestled into the hill, the pool house was given the look of a cottage in the woods to accentuate the rustic retreat look.

Low-maintenance plantings

Having your pool area ringed by a thick stand of trees boosts maintenance chores, but if the poolscape itself is designed for minimal upkeep, most of the work will occur in the late fall

Left: The dining terrace is slightly elevated from the pool deck. Rectangular, smooth-surface stones define this as a more formal area.

Below: Set into the base of the hill, the waterfall only appears to pour fresh, spring water into the pool.

and early spring, leaving your summers free to enjoy the water. This hideaway poolscape is a case in point. Although it appears to be a natural extension of the forest, its low-lying, small-leaved shrubs, perennials, and groundcovers have been positioned strategically, yet sparingly, to soften the stonework. All the trees stand well back from the pool and spa, behind a buffer zone of large shrubs and mulched slopes that will catch and hold a good portion of the leaves when they fall. Shade for the activity areas is provided by a canopy over the lounge area and an umbrella table on the dining terrace.

Pool Use and Maintenance

Tips for Smart Pool Care

Water in a mountain lake stays clear because it's continually replaced by fresh water flowing in; soiled water flows out. The water in your pool, however, isn't replaced constantly; it gets recycled many times. The only new water flowing in is the small amount needed to replace evaporation and splashing. Because a typical residential pool contains 30,000 gallons of water and because pool water acquires impurities whether or not it's used frequently, there needs to be a system for recycling all those gallons on a regular basis. Also, outdoor pools tend to collect debris from nature, so a pool's recycling system needs to remove the debris before it clogs the system or poses a health hazard. Here you'll get a basic understanding of how a system works, key points for selecting the system's components, and an overview of the basic equipment needed for routine pool maintenance.

Water in, water out

Initially, water reaches your pool via a pipe connected to your home's main water supply. Once the pool is filled, its plumbing becomes a closed system most of the time: Water enters your pool through inlets and exits through skimmers and drains. A pump creates the drive to suck the water into the drains and skimmers and to push it back into the pool through the inlets. Piping routes the water through a filter to remove tiny solids before returning the water to the pool. The filtered water also passes through a heater. The piping in the first half of the cycle is called suction piping; the piping in the second half is called return piping. The purpose of a skimmer is to trap surface debris. The purpose of a filter is to trap smaller particles. Pool drains are fitted with special grilles or grates designed to keep large objects (larger than $\frac{1}{2}$ inch wide) from being sucked into the drain pipe and to prevent swimmers from being trapped at the bottom of the pool by the drain's sucking action. Pool drains also are fitted with a hydrostatic valve, which allows groundwater to enter the pool if water-table pressure under the pool poses a hazard. Some circulation systems also include automatic water-treatment devices such as chlorine generators or ionization emitters to purify the water by killing most of the bacteria in it before returning it to the pool. Other water-treatment devices are portable units floating on the surface or attached to the side of the pool.

Good system, bad system

Sparkling, clear water is one sign that a pool system is purifying the water properly. To ensure a smooth-working system, choose durable, high-quality components matched with one another so no one component has to work overtime to keep everything running smoothly. Matching pipe size to flow rate and pumping power is a key factor in creating a well-balanced, long-lasting system. Piping for an average residential pool needs to be at least 2 inches in diameter. Smaller-diameter piping forces the pump to work harder, prematurely wearing out the pump. Be wary of dealers or contractors trying to sell a high-horsepower pump; if the piping is the right size, a standard

---

CALCULATING POOL VOLUME

To determine how much material to add when making adjustments in your pool's chemistry, you need to know its total volume in cubic feet. Here are some typical pool shapes and the formulas used for calculating their volumes:

Compute your pool's depth. Figure the average depth at the deep end and the average depth at the shallow end, then add the two numbers and divide by two to get your pool's average depth.

Rectangular or square pool. Multiply length × width × average depth × 7.5.

Oval pool. Multiply short diameter × long diameter × average depth × 5.9.

Circular pool. Multiply diameter × diameter × average depth × 5.9.

Free-form pool. Figure the average length and width and multiply according to the formula for rectangular pools.

one-horsepower pump will work perfectly. For larger pools, or those with special pump-driven features such as spas, fountains, and waterfalls, you may need a pump with more horsepower. If so, the piping should be 3-inches in diameter instead of 2 inches.

Picking the right products

When shopping for a pool pump, look for units that offer energy efficiency, quiet operation, a dual-speed option, and a two- or three-year warranty (versus one year). If an efficiency rating isn't provided by the manufacturer, you can calculate it yourself by dividing the number of gallons the unit pumps per hour by the unit's electrical power rating, which is usually stated in kilowatts. The higher the number that results, the more efficient the unit is. Also, look for a UL listing (Underwriters Laboratories), which indicates that the unit's design has been tested rigorously by an independent laboratory.

When selecting a pool filter, weigh personal preferences against practical considerations. Three basic types of pool filters are available. The most common type is the *sand filter,* which traps small particles by filtering water through a layer of fine-grain sand. Sand filters are relatively inexpensive, easy to operate, and can be reused many times. They're flushed out in a process called backwashing. Backwashing, however, requires a large volume of water. Another drawback is that sand filters can't remove extremely small particles (less than 15 microns, or the width of a human hair) so pool water never looks crystal clear. A *DE filter* uses fabric-covered grids coated with a thin layer of diatomaceous earth. Composed of tiny fossilized plant skeletons ground to a fine powder, this substance traps particles only 3 microns wide. DE filters are used widely but are more expensive than sand filters. Also, in certain locales, disposal of used DE material by flushing it out in the backwash is outlawed because DE tends to clog waste lines. *Cartridge filters* clean the water by filtering it through cartridges made of fine pleated mesh. Unlike sand and DE filters, cartridges don't require backwashing and can remove particles only 5–10 microns wide. However, they are more

expensive and need occasional cleaning. Each time they're cleaned, they lose 25 to 35 percent of their effectiveness so they need to be replaced after a couple cleanings.

To maintain a comfortable water temperature (78–98.6 degrees F), you need a heater. Even moderate heating can be expensive. Most residential pools in the United States are heated with electricity, oil, or gas (natural or propane). Gas heaters cost about $2,000. However, a few locales—mostly in the Sunbelt states—have mandated the use of solar-panel heaters, some of which are very moderately priced ($300 on up) but expensive to install. The least expensive pool-heating source is natural gas.

Several things will reduce heating costs. Locate your pool where it will be protected from strong or steady winds. Wind greatly accelerates evaporation of pool water, and a pool loses 60 percent of its heat through evaporation. Also, add a pool cover. All covers help hold in heat, and solar covers actually collect and add heat. Another good cost-saver is to lower the pool's thermostat 10 degrees when the pool won't be in use for several days. Or, install a heater that generates heat in a slow, continuous, energy-efficient manner instead of heating rapidly on demand. Examples are a solar-panel heater and a ground-source heat-pump heater. The disadvantage is that they're slow to recover from sharp changes in water temperature caused by refilling or by daily or seasonal weather patterns and therefore are impractical except in very mild climates.

Pool-Water Care

Keeping your pool water clean, clear, and safe is a delicate balancing act, one that requires regular attention. Water chemistry involves a blend of several different components, such as hardness (calcium content), pH, and total dissolved solids (TDS). It also involves pathogen content (bacteria). When the water components are out of balance, the result can cause damage to the pool shell or pool equipment or can promote growth of bacteria and algae, causing various health problems for swimmers and making the pool unsafe.

When done on a daily or weekly basis, pool maintenance requires a relatively small amount of time and effort, but you need to make it part of your routine. Even if you hire a pool service to make regular house calls, you still need to check the pump's strainer pot, clear debris from the skimmers and strainer baskets, check the pool filter to see if it needs cleaning or replacing, and test the water balance every few days. Pool water can go out of balance quickly and become a breeding ground for bacteria and algae whether or not the pool is used, but these changes happen even more quickly during periods of heavy use. Also, all these factors tend to be interdependent; treating the water to bring one component back in sync may throw others further out of balance. However, after some practice, you'll develop a feel for what needs to be done and how often.

Common problems

One telltale sign of unbalanced or unhealthy water chemistry is a greenish, brownish, or blackish discoloration in the water. The cause may be algae or excess dissolved metals from corroding fixtures. Another sign is cloudy or murky water, which usually means insufficient filtration. A third sign, more common in spas than in pools, is a buildup of powdery white deposits, called scale, above the waterline. In addition to visual clues such as these, some problems can be detected by using your nose. A strong musty odor indicates excess bacteria or algae growth. Strong chlorine odor indicates a deficiency of free active chlorine, which is the odorless, sanitizing form of chlorine that kills and oxidizes (burns) bacteria.

Filtering

The chief remedy for murky or discolored water is filtration. When you fill your pool for the first time, or when you refill it after draining and repairing or cleaning the shell, it's best to cycle the water through the filter continuously for at least 24 hours (some pool technicians recommend 72 hours). After that, begin reducing the run time in one-hour increments until you notice a decrease in water clarity. If your pool equipment is properly sized, it should recycle all the water at least once every 8 hours. When the water is properly recycled, you should be able to clearly see the drains at the bottom of the pool. For best results, develop a schedule that includes several on/off cycles during each 24-hour period, rather than a single filtering period followed by a long lull. During periods of busy pool use, you may need to filter more often. To simplify the task of maintaining a regular schedule, you may want to install an automatic timer on your pool pump.

Balancing

The ability of water to breed bacteria or to corrode metal surfaces depends on its total alkalinity and its pH reading. Total alkalinity is the amount of alkaline material in the water. When it is too high or too low, the pool water is out of balance. An acceptable level of alkaline material is between 80 and 150 parts per million. Another major balancing factor is the pH reading itself, which measures the water's relative alkalinity and acidity. The scale for reading pH levels ranges from 0 to 14, with proper (balanced) levels falling between 7.2 and 7.8. Water that's too alkaline (a high pH reading) results in scale deposits on equipment, pool walls, and plumbing; it also accelerates growth of bacteria and algae. Water that's too acidic (a low pH reading) allows chlorine sanitizers to dissipate too easily and causes metal parts to corrode quickly. Various types of inexpensive, easy-to-use kits are available for testing total alkalinity and pH levels. Baking soda or soda ash is used to raise alkalinity; muriatic acid or sodium bisulfate is used to lower it. These substances and test kits are available at your local pool supply dealer. Chemicals needed for balancing are added to the pool water near the outlets, never near the inlets; concentrations of these substances harm the pool filter or pump components.

Besides total alkalinity and pH level, other factors can also eventually affect the balance of your pool water and cause telltale clouding, algae growth, stains, or corrosion. Once or twice a year, take a sample of your pool water to a pool supply store and have it tested for calcium hardness, total dissolved solids, and cyanuric acid (a special conditioner that shields chlorine from ultraviolet light). As these water components build up over time, they hamper your pool's ability to maintain or restore a proper pH level. Usually, the only remedy is to drain the pool and refill it with fresh water.

Sanitizing and oxidizing

When your pool water is in balance, it's able to provide a stable medium for the chemicals needed to kill and/or oxidize (burn away) bacteria. There are a number of different ways to kill bacteria—not all of which involve chemicals—but no matter which method you use, you still need to use chemicals to burn off the dead organisms so they don't simply accumulate and cause a pollution problem of a different sort. Chlorine, the one used in most residential pools, works both as a sanitizer and as an oxidizer. It's available in several forms (gas, liquid, granules, and tablets), but the two that are used most widely are liquid chlorine and tablet chlorine. Liquid chlorine is usually poured directly into the pool water; tablet chlorine is usually dispensed gradually through a mechanical feeder. Although it is

dual-purpose, the amount of chlorine needed for sanitizing is often insufficient for complete oxidation; before the chlorine has a chance to oxidize all the dead microorganisms in the water, it combines with nitrogen (another common impurity in pool water) to form chloramines. Chloramines inhibit sanitization and cause the strong odor associated with chlorine. When too many chloramines form, the pool needs super-chlorinating, or shocking.

Like chlorine, bromine is a good sanitizer, but it is unstable in sunlight and works best in higher-temperature water, so it's more commonly used in spas. Several effective alternatives to chlorine are available for sanitizing pools. They range from simple, low-tech options such as salt tablets to high-tech devices such as ozone generators and ultraviolet light-beam chambers. Although most are initially more expensive than installing a chemical feeder or adding chlorine by hand, they simplify the treatment process and drastically reduce the amount of chlorine needed.

Below: Test pool water regularly to ensure its purity.

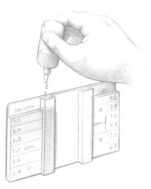

Cleaning and Checking

Besides applying some basic chemistry, regular maintenance on your pool will involve a bit of elbow grease and inspection. An arsenal of basic hand tools will prove invaluable in dealing with each type of chore. In some cases the tool you use depends on the pool shell.

Some of the debris that falls into a pool settles to the bottom or catches in the skimmer baskets or in the pump's strainer pot and is removed by hand or by sucking it up with a vacuum tool. Some also simply floats on the water's surface and has to be retrieved with a net. In addition, pools develop a bathtub ring near the waterline—a thin layer of scum that builds up from body oils and tanning lotions and scale deposits (calcium carbonate). The scum must be scrubbed off regularly with a solution of 1 part muriatic acid and 5 parts tile soap. Stubborn areas may need to be loosened with a pumice block. Scale deposits must be loosened and scrubbed away with stainless-steel brushes. It's also important to remove algae, which tend to grow on the sides and bottom of the pool when the pool water isn't properly balanced.

You can slash your maintenance time in half by doing some of this work with labor-saving partly or totally automated gadgetry. Ordinary pool vacuums must be guided across the pool's bottom by hand, and the suction is generated by a garden hose. A robotic vacuum cleaner, on the other hand, is electric; you put it in the pool, turn it on, and it just prowls the floor of the pool, sucking up debris. (The pool can't be used while the vacuum is operating.) For total, hands-free vacuuming, install a built-in system. Although labor-saving devices such as these are much costlier than conventional hand tools, they boost enjoyment of a pool considerably and reduce other types of pool maintenance costs, including those of a professional pool-service technician.

Follow a logical sequence

To avoid repeating the same task during a given maintenance session, do your chores in a particular sequence, following the path the water takes through the circulation system. Start by skimming off surface debris and scrubbing down the waterline area. Clean out the skimmer baskets, then shut off the pump and clean out the basket in the pump's strainer pot. Reprime the pump and check the pressure on the filter. (If it's 10 pounds above normal, the filter probably is clogged and needs backwashing or replacing.) Then sweep the pool sides with a nylon broom and vacuum the floor. Finally, test the water chemistry for balance.

When doing maintenance, inform everyone in your household that the pool is off-limits—even during periods when all the hands-on chores are done and the pool water is simply recycling to achieve balance. Establish an easily recognizable "pool closed" mode, such as turning all the outdoor furniture upside down or erecting a removable security fence and posting signs on the fence. Keep in mind that occasionally you may need to close the pool for at least

Below: 1. A buoyant, vinyl-coated tube can be hooked around a victim, with a tow rope at one end and a hook fastener at the other.
2. A long-handled, lightweight pole with a crook on one end lassoes victims who are floundering, floating, or drifting underwater.
3. A buoyant ring is tossed to a victim who is still conscious and can grab hold; at all times the ring should be securely fastened to a safety rope that will reach at least halfway across the pool.

3. Ring buoy

1. Rescue tube

2. Shepard's crook

24 hours—or as long as 72 hours—to give the water chemistry ample time to achieve proper balance. Improperly balanced water can pose a serious health hazard to swimmers, potentially causing skin rashes and eye irritations.

Other safety measures

Basic pool safety measures should become an integral part of your family's routine when the pool is in use. In addition to maintaining constant supervision, keep a first-aid kit and basic lifesaving aids close at hand. Each family member should have CPR and water safety training and know how to float, if they don't know how to swim. If you plan to use your pool for entertaining relatives and friends, they will need some clear guidelines to avoid unfortunate mishaps. Therefore, consider drawing up a set of basic rules for pool use at your house (see sample list of rules in box, page 81) and posting them in plain view near the pool so everyone has ample opportunity to refer to them and conduct themselves accordingly.

1. Concrete pool vacuum

2. Tile brush

6. Wall/floor brush

3. Leaf skimmer

5. Algae brush

4. Vinyl-lined pool vacuum

Left: 1. A concrete pool vacuum works like the vinyl-lined pool vacuum but has stiffer bristles. 2. A stiff-bristle brush removes scale deposits. 3. A long-handled, lightweight scoop fitted with a mesh net gathers surface debris. 4. Bristles loosen dirt that is then sucked through the hose into one of the pool's skimmers. 5. Stainless-steel bristles remove algae from tile- or plaster-lined pools. 6. Nylon bristles sweep debris off pool walls and across the pool floor toward drains.

Left: Automated pool cleaners use your pool's pumping system to suck up dirt and debris and/or drive it toward the pool filter via drains and skimmers. Some types plug into the pool skimmers; another type, built into the pool floor, contains jets that work directly off the pumping system.

Hot Tubs and Spas

You can enjoy the pleasures of steamy, bubbly hot water at the touch of a button.

For many people, the pleasure of a relaxing soak in steamy hot water equals, or even surpasses, those of plunging into a cool swimming pool. Fortunately, to enjoy the luxury of soaking away the tensions, aches, and pains of daily life, you no longer have to journey far away to a sanitarium or an exclusive resort. Thanks to a series of technological innovations that began to appear in the late 1960s, you can install a private hot-spring spa in your own backyard—or even in your bedroom.

Referred to interchangeably as a hot tub or a spa, the modern version of this time-honored form of relaxation and therapy has proven amazingly versatile and practical. It's an ideal complement for backyard pools as well as a stand-alone amenity—especially for yards that are too small to accommodate a pool. And its compact size and shape make it a perfect candidate for indoor locations.

Whether you're thinking of including a hot tub or spa in your pool scheme right away or adding it later as an upgrade, or installing it in lieu of a pool, this chapter gives you the basic technical and design considerations. The following pages also highlight new product options being offered by this extremely fast-growing segment of the home recreation industry.

Like its wood-tub counterparts, this built-in spa features a classic circular shape and a rustic, naturalistic character that merges seamlessly with the lush greenery nearby. The wide stone ledge that forms its rim makes it easy to perch while climbing in or out of the water.

Pick Your Pleasure: Hot Tub or Spa

The passion for soaking in steamy waters to relieve tension or cure various physical ills spans the globe and dates back to ancient times. Hot springs in southern England prompted the Romans to build elaborate baths there in 50 A.D. To this day, the English city of Bath continues to draw throngs of people seeking to "partake of the waters." Archeologists have unearthed structures of similar age in Japan; there are still public baths in modern-day Japan. Japanese homes often include a cubelike furo, a one-person version of the American hot tub.

In the United States, an industry grew out of the 1960s hot tub craze in Northern California's wine country, when members of the counterculture movement began slicing discarded wine casks in half and converting them to tubs for communal soaking. Barrel-makers began making tubs specifically for use as home hot tubs. Still manufactured on a small scale, hot tubs are available in several types of rot-resistant wood—cedar, teak, and mahogany as well as traditional redwood. Coopering (barrelmaking) is more a craft than an industrial process, and because the kiln-dried wood must be clear, vertical-grain heartwood—increasingly scarce in certain species—solid-wood hot tubs are quite expensive. A new tub made of heart redwood costs between $1,000 and $3,000. If given proper care, a well-made tub lasts at least 15 years.

Regular maintenance for a wood tub filled with hot water is essential because the surfaces and seams of the wood offer thousands of tiny crevices where bacteria can lodge. Keeping the water sanitized is

Above: Prefabricated spas are available as portable units or as drop-in shells for permanent inground or on-deck installations. They can also be custom-built on site. Many spas are mounted in thickly insulated cabinets and protected by insulated covers so water can be kept warm—and heated quickly and economically.

For those who consider themselves purists when it comes to hot-water relaxation and therapy, the only choice is a hot tub. Strictly speaking, a hot tub is a large wooden barrel cut in half and filled with heated water. It may or may not have hydrojets (special fittings that mix air and water and inject them under pressure to add force and swirl to the water), and only the larger versions (holding between 500 and 850 gallons of water) have built-in benches. Their almost primitive simplicity is a large part of their appeal. So is the subtle musky scent that hot water draws out of the wood, and the feel of the wood against wet skin.

Characteristics of Hot Tubs

SHAPES	SIZES	ADVANTAGES	DRAWBACKS
Round	**Small:** Under 500 gallons; 3–4 feet high; 5-foot diameter; seats 2–3 people	Fits small spaces	Encourages bacterial growth
Oval		Rustic charm	Requires more frequent testing and treating
Square (furo)		Total immersion (up to the neck)	
	Large: 500+ gallons; 4–5 feet high; 6-foot diameter; seats 8–10 people	Noiseless (if used only for soaking)	Develops leaks if wood is allowed to dry out
		Feels warmer and softer against bare skin	

much harder than in a smooth-surfaced pool, so some wood tubs come with an acrylic liner. This sleek inner shell is easier to keep clean than natural wood and most bacteria find it harder to take hold. Both types need more frequent testing, treating, and cleaning than a swimming pool because the impurities in a tub are much more concentrated. (Three people soaking in a hot tub is equivalent to 100 people swimming in an average-size pool.) Unsanitary water poses a serious health hazard to bathers, and unbalanced water will accelerate wood rot.

Spa essentials

If you're concerned more with comfort and convenience than with rustic charm and authenticity, your best option may be a spa. Often referred to as hot tubs—even by spa dealers—there are important characteristics that set spas apart from their wood-barrel cousins. Spas are shallower than tubs and built-in seating is in an inclined position, whereas seating in a hot tub is upright on a simple bench—or the tub floor. All spas are equipped with hydrojets, whereas most hot tubs have none at all and offer only soaking in still water. Finally, the outer shell of a spa may or may not be real wood, while a hot tub is, by definition, a cylinder of solid wood staves held together with steel bands.

While hot tubs have remained a small, very specialized, region-specific industry, spas have become a diversified, broadly dispersed, highly technical industry of mass production. Since the late 1960s, home-spa buyers have been treated to an endless succession of innovative features that merge the basic spa concept with water-recreation and hydrotherapy technologies. An example is the swim-spa (see pages 96–97) that combines soaking and massage with swim-in-place workouts. The latest refinements use electronics and synthetic materials to create more enjoyable and convenient experiences—push-button hydrojet controls, digital programmable lighting, and built-in stereo surround-sound systems. In short, hot tubs are still an essentially simple form of hot-water therapy and relaxation; spas have evolved into highly sophisticated, intricately engineered home-recreation appliances.

Factory-built spas range from $3,000 to $8,000, still a good value for a product that can be enjoyed more months of the year than an outdoor pool. They make a perfect activity for companions and are even more inviting when the weather is cool.

Above: The rustic character of wood tubs makes them look perfectly at home in naturalistic settings. Both tubs and spas are compact enough for tiny backyards, indoor locations, and even apartment balconies, but spas offer a broader range of installation options.

Characteristics of Spas

SHAPES	SIZES	ADVANTAGES	DRAWBACKS
Round Oval Octagon Rectangle Square Freeform	**Smallest:** 230 gallons; 29 inches high; 6-foot diameter; seats 4 people **Largest:** 800 gallons; 40 inches high, 8 feet wide, 10 feet long; seats 6–8 people	Fits in small spaces Sleek, easy-care finishes Built-in seating Year-round usability Several installation options Wide variety of shapes and sizes	Requires more frequent testing and treating than a pool does Not deep enough for total-immersion soaking

Factory-Built Spas & Options

If one-of-a-kind design isn't a prime concern in the planning of your spa, you'll find a number of factory-built spas that offer all the features on your wish list, plus some extras. What you get in place of custom design is one-stop shopping convenience, name-brand quality assurance, and the advantages of buying a complete package—including warranties and service provided by the manufacturer and the dealer. Although selection is limited to whatever is listed in the catalogs or on the showroom floor at a given time, the range of choices industrywide is surprisingly broad and varied.

Standard features

At a glance, many factory-built units look alike and share certain basic features that have become standard. The vast majority are constructed of acrylic or thermoplastic shells molded to form one-piece tub units with built-in seating. Some, however, have plywood/backerboard shells faced with tile or stone. Many factory-builts are designed as freestanding portable units that you can move indoors or outdoors as the seasons change, and even take with you when you move to another address. Others are designed as drop-in units for permanent outdoor or indoor installations, such as gazebos, terraces, decks, pool areas, sunrooms, and basements. In both portable or drop-in spas, the list of standard features includes several hydrojets, a built-in skimmer, several air-blower inlets (also called bubblers), a pump, a filter, and a heater (usually electric for portables and gas for drop-ins). Most units also feature a single or dual floor drain.

Shop around

Unlike their wooden counterparts, factory-built spas come in many shapes, sizes, and colors. Some manufacturers offer a full spectrum of choices, from simple round units to elaborate octagonal designs. Other manufacturers specialize in one basic shape but offer it in numerous sizes with various levels of upgrade amenities. If several dealers are

POOL & SPA POINTERS

These are just a few of the many options to choose from when you order a factory-built spa. Depending on the manufacturer, some may be standard items; others are special accessories or upgrades that you order separately.
- Push-button control panel
- Built-in refreshment tray
- Padded headrests
- Fountains
- Decorative lighting
- Built-in stereo system
- Fragrances (liquid or crystal)
- Built-in water-testing component

located in your area, do a little footwork and visit the showrooms in person before narrowing the field to a single product line. Attend home-remodeling shows, where local dealers and large manufacturers usually exhibit their latest spa products. And check out the ads in home improvement magazines and on spa manufacturers' websites; many companies market their products coast to coast and may have recently acquired a dealer or distributor near you.

Take the wet test

Showroom visits are particularly important because they give you a chance to see firsthand the special features available with a specific product line, the degree of quality and durability incorporated into each model, and the level of service you can expect from the dealership once you sign on the dotted line. During such visits, do not let the roomful of shiny new spa units, arrayed in dazzling metallic finishes, intimidate you. All that glitz may be little more than glamorous packaging for an inferior product. One feature to look for is adjustable hydrojets. When it comes to hydromassage, a few jets that direct the flow of water exactly where it will provide the most benefit are much more useful than more fixed jets that don't target the right spots. Look also for a diverter valve that allows you to shift the main force of the jetting system from one area of the spa to another—a handy option when you need extra massage after an especially strenuous workout. Don't be bashful about taking showroom units for a test run. Most dealers encourage this, in fact, by providing changing rooms on site so you can wet-test their products—try them out with water in them and the jets turned on. Wet or dry, test the seating to see if you can sit comfortably without having to slouch down in order to immerse yourself up to your shoulders or to gain firm footing and to see if the seating provides proper lumbar support for your back.

Check out the systems

Examine each unit's technical aspects with a critical eye. Check the warm-up time on the

WORKING WITH A DEALER

When it comes to purchasing, installing, and maintaining your new spa, a reputable spa dealer can save you a lot of time and inconvenience up front and down the road. A well-established, full-service dealer will secure building permits (if necessary), do the installation, and provide routine service. He or she may also repair a damaged shell or help coordinate repair work that is provided by the manufacturer. Some spa dealers also sell and install pools, and in some cases spas may be little more than a sideline. Make sure your dealer has been in the spa business for several years and can give good references. When you visit a showroom, look for plaques, seals, or other indications that the dealer is affiliated with trade organizations that promote good customer service and quality products. Examples include Underwriter's Laboratories (UL) listings and the seal of approval of the International Association of Plumbers and Mechanical Officials (I.A.P.M.O). Be sure to read all the fine print in the dealer's warranties, which usually are printed on one page of each of the product brochures that are handed out to customers. To locate dealers in your area, look for listings in the phone book under "Hot Tubs" or "Spas." Also check local listings for pool or spa designers and ask them for the names of dealers they would recommend in your area.

heater; units with small heaters actually waste energy rather than conserve it because they burn up extra power trying to raise or maintain the water temperature. Another energy-saving consideration is insulation, particularly regarding aboveground spas (portables). Look for a full-foam insulated cabinet in these units. Also, check the filter size; the minimum size for a three-person spa is a filter that contains 100 square feet of filtering membrane. And compare the noise levels of various models when the jets and pump are turned on; quiet operation will ensure a more relaxing soak—and the ability to converse in a normal tone when you share the spa with family and friends.

Read the fine print

Finally, take a close look at the warranties and service agreements offered by the dealer and/or manufacturer. Will any surface imperfections on the shell be repaired by the dealer or by a factory representative? Whose responsibility is it to remove the unit if it needs to be sent in for repairs? A good warranty usually covers the cost of parts, plumbing, and labor on a spa unit for five years. Warranties on the heater, skimmer, air blowers, filter—support equipment—vary from one to three years.

Portable Spas

Originally intended as a lower-maintenance alternative to the wooden hot tub, portable spas have all but eclipsed their rustic, barrel-shaped predecessors in popularity and market share. Today, only about 1 percent of home spas are the genuine wood-tub variety; most spa owners seem to prefer the flexibility, affordability, and special amenities available in a broad range of portable spa products.

Portable spas feature a molded plastic shell that's much easier to keep clean than natural wood. In most portables, the shell is made from a sheet of ⅛-inch-thick acrylic plastic that is vacuum-formed inside a female mold and then strengthened on the underside with a layer of fiberglass. In higher-quality units and those that require extra rigidity because of their holding capacity, the shell may be vacuum-formed thermoplastic, a durable material that by itself is stronger than acrylic, with a fiberglass backing. A typical unit seats two to three people. It has a depth of 26 inches and weighs about 300 pounds empty, so it can be turned on its side and carried into the house through a standard-size entry door. When filled, it weighs about 2,500 pounds, so it may require extra structural support if installed indoors. Portable units are mounted in cabinets made of wood or rigid polymers. Good-quality units are filled with a thick layer of foam insulation that fills the space inside the cabinet between the shell and the skirting. This allows the unit to be left outdoors in cold weather with the water kept constantly warm without wasting energy. Properly insulated, an average-size portable unit costs about $1 per day to operate.

Quick hookup

Ease of installation is another advantage that accounts for the portable spa's widespread

popularity. Unlike in-ground spas, a portable doesn't require a building permit. And all but the largest units can simply be set in place and plugged into a 110-volt outlet like an ordinary household appliance. However, the outlet needs to be connected to a dedicated 20-amp circuit, with no other appliances using that circuit. Large units (those seating six to eight people) need to be hardwired to a 220-volt dedicated circuit. Portables require no permanent household plumbing connections; you fill them with a garden hose.

When you select a location for a portable spa, remember that the unit needs to sit on a firm foundation that can support the combined weight of the spa, the water, and the people using it. An inadequate foundation may shift, causing the shell to split or crack or the mechanical system to spring a leak. Damage caused by foundation problems isn't covered by spa warranties.

Cabinet options

For several decades, the cabinets made for portable spas were clad with natural wood, a carryover from the original wood hot tub. Natural wood skirting remains an option, with redwood still the most common type. However, in an effort to meet consumer demands for minimum maintenance and long-term durability, many manufacturers have switched to no-rot synthetic materials for skirting, such as rigid polymers or thermoplastics. Some of these nonwood options have a convincing wood look; others are purposefully high-tech to complement the sleek, space-age finishes of the shells they enclose. Whichever type you choose, make sure that the skirting fits snugly, hangs vertically, and, in the case of real wood, is made of heartwood that is at least $\frac{1}{2}$ inch thick. If you do choose wood, it will need restaining once a year to look its best and to minimize potential damage from moisture and weather.

Accessories galore

Portable spas come in a broad range of shapes and sizes, from simple circular units

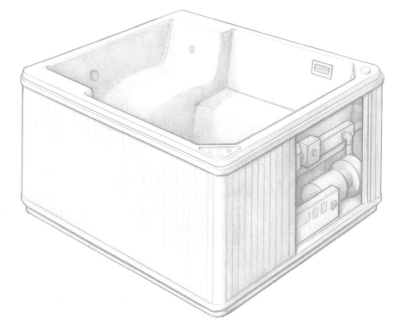

to highly convoluted octagonals. Many accessories and luxury features are available to pick from, depending on the manufacturer, dealer, and/or model. For example, almost all companies offer at least one model featuring multiple hydrojet massage areas, either a general massage area plus a special therapy alcove or several specialty massage options intermingled with the general hydrojet action. Some specialty areas concentrate on neck massage; others concentrate on lumbar areas or on calves and feet.

Other common accessories include a set of steps and a deck, refreshment bar, privacy screen, built-in refreshment tray, master diverter valve, or push-button control panel. Even a brief tour of local spa showrooms will yield a host of appealing options, such as a built-in digital pH readout for the water treatment system, a plug-in vacuum tool for sucking up debris from the shell bottom, fiberoptic accent lighting that highlights the outer and inner rim of the shell at night, and an elegant wood gazebo that you erect from a kit to provide privacy and wind protection. One spa manufacturer even offers a portable unit that features its own built-in infinity edge.

Above: As this cutaway drawing illustrates, the typical portable spa is a self-contained unit, with a skimmer built into the shell and a skid pack (support equipment) housed in a compartment behind the cabinet's skirting. In a good-quality unit, the rest of the cabinet cavity is filled with foam insulation and the skirting is either heartwood or no-rot, rigid polymer panels.

Built-In Spas

Originally, all spas were permanent, built-in facilities—either small- or large-scale inground pools filled with naturally or artificially heated water. These built-ins remain a popular option for homeowners who prefer an integrated, settled-in look or who want the freedom to determine the size, shape, and design of their spa. Much of the technology that spurred development of portable spas has made built-in spas more affordable and user-friendly too.

Built-in versus portable

A built-in spa is permanently installed either inground or above ground (such as on a patio, a deck, or in an indoor space). It

may be either fully or partly recessed into the surface that surrounds it, and it may rest on a concrete footing or on a sand base within an excavation. A portable unit always sits on a flat surface that gives the necessary support. Equipment for a built-in is located away from the unit (as pool equipment is) whereas equipment for a portable is inside the unit. Electrical power for a built-in unit is hardwired to a dedicated, 220-volt circuit; all but the largest portables are plugged into a 110-volt outlet (on a dedicated circuit). The support system (circulation, filtering, and heating equipment) for a built-in is integrated with the pool's support system; in a portable, it is self-contained and pre-installed.

Advantages and drawbacks

The main advantages of a built-in unit are aesthetic. Much of the unit's bulk is out of view, so there is no need for accessories such as removable steps or clip-on refreshment bars. The installation has a streamlined look and the surrounding area is more open. Also, built-ins don't require a factory-built cabinet; they rest inside a site-built casing or excavation either totally concealed under the unit or designed to match surrounding surfaces. A totally site-built spa can be a one-of-a-kind design statement.

Built-ins offer practical advantages as well. They are quieter than portables; when the equipment is operating, motor noise and vibration are isolated behind a fence or inside a shed. The recessed design makes it easier to get in and out of the water. The ledge that surrounds a built-in unit is always site-built and can be wide enough to perch on while swinging your legs in or out. In a totally recessed unit, the ledge is part of the surrounding floor, deck, or paved area itself.

One drawback of built-ins is the much longer lead time for installation. Once a portable is delivered to the site, it can be used within hours, whereas installation of a built-in may take several weeks. Built-in installations are generally more expensive because they involve custom design and skilled construction labor. A factory-built shell costs less, but you'll still need technical and design expertise and job supervision on site. You must obtain a building permit, and the work must pass all inspections.

Shopping for a shell

Built-in spas offer many more options for shells than portables do. The shells of many factory-built units are made of vacuum-formed acrylic backed with fiberglass. Some units are made of only fiberglass; others are made of thermoplastic or a plywood/backer-board/fiberglass sandwich faced with tile or

polished stone. The latter is often made to order rather than mass-produced and has one clear advantage—its solid, masonry-sheathed, site-built look. A disadvantage—to some owners and designers, at least—is that the shell is mainly rectangular with only slight curves, if any. Another, strictly on-site, option is reinforced concrete (gunite or shotcrete) surfaced with plaster, tile, fiber-glass, aggregate, or stone. Gunite or shotcrete is usually the material of choice for homeowners who want a totally built-in look and have the budgets for custom-designed, site-built spas. Many want the pool and spa to have identical finishes, shapes, and edge treatments in the shells and deck areas.

One other option for the spa shell is poured, reinforced concrete (versus blown-in). This process involves setting plywood forms and reinforcing rods and then pouring concrete into the forms. After the concrete has set and the forms are removed, the concrete is left to cure and then finished with a layer of plaster. Once used widely, poured concrete is out of favor because free-form shapes and rounded corners are so difficult to construct. Regular concrete mix tends to leach chemicals into the water when the spa is first filled, causing stains in the plastic coating and requiring multiple refills before the spa can be used safely.

Shopping for a support system

Although the support system for an inground unit isn't built into the unit, spa dealers usually sell and install both the shell and the equipment as a package (called a skid pack). But whether you buy your equipment as a package or in individual components, ask the same questions raised on page 91. Check how fast the water heats, how much area (in square feet) the filter car-tridges contain, and whether the skid-pack components are matched electronically and hydraulically to each other and to the spa. Does the unit have seals of approval from national testing laboratories, and does the fine print in the warranties and service agreements seem fair? Note that larger units (more than 350 gallons) need at least two pumps—one for the hydrojets and bubblers and one for water circulation and filtering. Units with numerous pump-driven special features, such as waterfalls, fountains, or swim jets, should have at least four pumps. It's best to buy a built-in unit equipped with fully adjustable jets and a diverter valve for optimum control of the water action.

Water Workouts

Although hydrojet technology was originally invented as a means of treating tired or injured muscles and ligaments, its uses have broadened in recent years. Nowhere is the change more dramatic than in the home pool and spa industry, where the resistance created by jetted water is now being used as a means of exercising in water, not just relaxing or recuperating. Aerobic and muscle-toning routines such as jogging and stair-stepping, activities once done only at health clubs, can now be done at home in a pool or spa.

New breed of products

A host of hybrid products has emerged to harness the potential of hydrojetted water. One device is the swim jet, a hydrojet installed in a new or existing swimming pool to generate a steady, adjustable current for swimming in place. Equipped with a pump and suction inlet, a self-contained swim jet system operates independently of the pool's circulation system. Swim jets offer an easy, cost-effective way to upgrade an average-size pool. For about $3,000, you can add swim-in-place technology to an existing or new pool.

If walking or jogging is more your style, you can do these in the water also. One device developed specifically for this is an aquatic treadmill, which resembles a conventional treadmill but is self-propelled and fully sealed to be operated under water. Like the swim jet, it enables you to exercise in place in a relatively small, shallow pool, to select a comfortable level of exertion, and to use the natural resistance of water to help build up stamina. The water's buoyancy provides low-impact cushioning for the body while you work out. Another means to achieve the same results is to use a spa deep enough at one end (4 to 8 feet) for jogging in place (see sketch, page 104). Hydrojets at the deep end function similar to a swim jet, generating an adjustable current so that you can jog continuously without bumping into the end of the unit. Other devices designed to turn your spa into an exercise machine include rowing oars that fit into ports in the sidewalls and weights that attach to ankles or wrists for performing underwater muscle-toning exercises.

Perhaps the most adaptable and versatile hybrid is the swim-spa. Part pool, part spa, part exercise machine, the swim-spa is a great choice if you like to swim laps but don't have room for a lap pool or a pool long enough for swimming laps. Equipped with swim jets plus additional jets for massaging and relaxing muscles, a swim-spa combines the functions of a spa and a lap pool in a unit anywhere from 10 to 20 feet long—less than half the length of an average swimming pool. Not only does a swim-spa take up less space than a lap pool, it's easier to use; because you swim in place against a current, there's no need to interrupt your stroke to dive and change direction. If the jets in your spa have adjustable power settings, each swimmer can adjust the current to match their ability. The smaller versions are single units that you use interchangeably for exercise or for hydrotherapy. Depending on their design or the placement of jets, some models will accommodate both activities at once. The water temperature needed for hydrotherapy isn't always suitable for strenuous exertion, so you may want to consider dual units—a swim-spa for exercise and a regular spa for hydrotherapy and relaxation. Most swim-spa manufacturers offer both single and dual units. Lengths for dual units vary from 16 to 20 feet, widths from 7 to 8 feet, and depths from

Below: A swim-spa takes advantage of water jets that produce a constantly moving current of water, allowing you to swim in place. The typical unit takes up less than half the length of an average swimming pool.

3 to 8 feet. Prices for single units start at about $9,000. For dual units, expect to pay between $12,000 and $15,000. Although costing more than the average-size conventional spa, a dual-unit swim-spa is still only half the cost of a full-size swimming pool, costs less to maintain (it contains only half as much treated water), and can be used virtually year-round.

Despite the fact that swim-spas are still relative newcomers to the pool and spa industry, they're already available in a variety of types and materials. Many are one-piece units of vacuum-molded acrylic or thermoplastic, but others have panelized shells (steel, aluminum, or rigid polymer) with vinyl liners. Some are designed as aboveground units with polymer- or wood-skirted cabinets; others are drop-in units that fit flush with a deck surface (either indoors or outdoors). Like regular spas, the aboveground units usually come with built-in skid packs and can be fitted with lockable, insulated covers.

Buying tips

Whether you prefer to exercise in a hydrotherapy spa, a single-unit swim-spa, or a dual-unit swim-spa, keep several considerations in mind as you visit showrooms and websites to compare products. First, look for a unit that offers plenty of room to stretch out, with full depth from side to side in the center portion of the shell, the area where you do most of your exercise. Many units stairstep inward on the sides, leaving only a narrow pocket of full-depth water in the center and creating obstructions that interfere with exercises such as rowing, swimming in place, and muscle-toning. Units with steps at one end usually offer more full-depth space in the middle. Second, check to see how many pumps are included in the skid pack. If you plan to use your spa for exercise as well as hydrotherapy, or if you want to install a swim-spa, you need a unit larger than the average home spa. For larger spas, you should install at least two pumps—one for

> ### BENEFITS OF A WATER WORKOUT
> Working out in a pool or spa is widely recognized by medical experts as a safe, effective, nonmedicinal method of treating common physical ailments—many of which accompany the natural process of aging—such as arthritis, back pain, tension, muscle or nerve damage, and insomnia. One advantage of underwater workouts is that they exercise all the major muscle groups simultaneously, regardless of your exercise routine. Another benefit is that the body becomes 90 percent lighter when suspended in water, so exercises have a gentle, low-impact effect on joints and contact areas. However, water workouts aren't safe for everyone. Before you begin a regular regimen of exercise, consult your family doctor to find out how to proceed.

circulating and filtering the water and one for the hydrojets and air blowers (bubblers). For spas with an unusual number of jets and bubblers and for swim-spas, it's best to have at least three pumps—one for circulation and filtering, one for hydrojets and blowers, and one for swimjets. If the unit also includes a fountain, a waterfall, or several swim jets, you may need a fourth pump.

Another key consideration when comparing larger spas is the heating equipment. Electric heaters are not a smart choice for large units; look instead for spas with natural-gas or propane heaters, preferably ones with electronic ignition rather than standing pilot lights.

If shopping for a swim-spa, look for units equipped with fully adjustable swimjets—ones that allow you to adjust the speed of the current and also the direction. Speed is adjusted by selecting a different pump setting on the control panel; the direction is adjusted by rotating the jet nozzle. Jets with fixed nozzles can't be adjusted to suit your needs. Also look for units with shells designed to control any backwash, the turbulence caused when a swimjet current bounces off the other end of the spa. If not absorbed or trapped at that end, backwash can interfere with the swimmer's rhythm or prevent the use of other areas of the spa while the swimjets are running. Another factor affecting the unit's swim-factor is the number and placement of the swimjets. A well-equipped swim-spa should have four swimjets: two directed toward the swimmer (one at each shoulder, for lateral stability) and two directed toward the bottom of the unit so that their current deflects upward (to generate even more buoyancy).

Choose Your Location

The amount of time you spend enjoying your spa will depend largely on how well you've planned its location. If your spa is easily accessible—even during cold or rainy weather—and if the surroundings feel soothing and inviting, regular soaks or water workouts are more likely to become a daily routine. In addition to deciding on a general location, you should consider ways for creating a setting to enhance the experience. Also address practical matters such as maintenance, utility connections, safety, and security.

Outdoor spots

Because spas are generally more compact than pools, they offer more placement options. They can be indoors or outdoors, above ground or inground (or halfway between), integral with a pool or separate, enclosed within a gazebo or mounted on a deck. Many pool owners prefer a spa integrated with the pool, for conveniently alternating between refreshing dips and soothing soaks or for relaxing in the spa while supervising swimmers in the pool. An integral pool/spa combo is especially handy for entertaining large groups too. If you live in a cold, windy climate, you may want to install a stand-alone unit close to the house, unless your pool scheme will accommodate an integral spa within a few steps of your door. A spot near the pool that's comfortable in warm weather may be very disagreeable in other seasons, but a location near the house may offer protection. You may also need to add a fence or an enclosure to divert wind around your spa area.

Placing your spa adjacent to the house may not be the best alternative either. If the unit sits directly under an eave, runoff and melting ice on the roof may drop into the spa as you're soaking or may drop onto the

Right: This elegant, tile-lined spa doubles as a fountain and waterfall at one end of a pool. In addition to the pleasures of steamy, swirling water, users can enjoy refreshing sprays from the fountain and the soothing music of the waterfall.

cover and damage it when the unit is not in use. Avoid locations directly beneath large trees or ones that shed debris, or add a gazebo for protection.

Terrain may dictate the best site. Like pools, spas must sit perfectly level, and adjoining areas must have proper drainage. Often the level spots in a yard are close to the house; the farther out you go, the more the yard is likely to slope up or down and require more cutting or filling to achieve a level base.

There are other good reasons why a spot near the house is the most practical. Both portable and drop-in spas need to be near an electrical outlet, and drop-ins need a protected place close by to house the support equipment.

It's best to be near a shower and changing area (preferably indoors). Because spas are much smaller than pools, the bacteria, body oils, residues from lotions, and other impurities in the water are more concentrated; showering ahead of time keeps the water clean longer.

In many backyards, the area near the house offers the most privacy. If the house doesn't screen out views of neighbors' yards or windows, you may need to add a wall or privacy fence or to enclose the spa with screens or a gazebo. Shrubbery serves the same purpose, provided it doesn't lose its foliage.

To achieve optimum restorative or therapeutic benefits, many people prefer to soak or work out in secluded settings, surrounded by natural beauty and isolated from the hubbub of everyday life. If you feel this way, live in a mild climate, or plan to use your spa only during the warmer months, a location away from the house may be your best option. Supply power to the site by installing a buried cable; if your spa is a drop-in unit, you'll need a shed nearby to house the support equipment.

Indoor spots

If an indoor location has more appeal, set aside a separate enclosure for this purpose. Unlike a whirlpool tub, which is filled with steamy water only when in use, a spa remains filled and at least partially heated at all times. The space it occupies must be able

to adequately vent the resulting high humidity. Excess humidity causes condensation on walls, floors, and windows, which in turn can cause rust, dry rot, and mold (thought to be responsible for some serious lung conditions linked to indoor spas). Control methods include extra insulation; double- or triple-pane glazing in windows and doors; a vapor barrier under interior and exterior walls, the floor, and the ceiling; a floor drain to dispose of splashed water; and a ventilation system with strategically placed vents, duct fans, operable windows, and at least one operable skylight or roof window. Choose moisture-resistant finishes such as ceramic or terra-cotta tile or rot-resistant wood, and fill the room with moisture-loving plants.

Install an indoor spa near a shower and changing area, and away from noisy areas of the house. If the spa will be a place for the family or for entertaining friends, avoid locating it where others must pass through a bedroom to get to it.

Whether in existing space or added on, indoor spas usually require extra support. Most homes are designed to hold about 40 pounds per square foot; an average-size spa, filled with water and several people, however, weighs about 243 pounds per square foot. It should be supported separately from underneath, on its own foundation.

Above: A railing and a privacy screen give this deck-mounted drop-in spa a sense of enclosure. Although the spa appears to be part of the deck, it's supported separately on its own foundation.

Spa Use &
Maintenance

The steamy, swirling, bubbling waters that make a spa or hot tub so inviting for people also make an ideal environment for biological impurities to thrive and multiply. Typical conditions cause water to lose its chemical balance easily, becoming either too alkaline or too acidic. Water heated between 100 degrees and 104 degrees F—the recommended range for spas and hot tubs—is ideal for the growth of bacteria and algae. The extra evaporation caused by heating and water movement accelerates the loss of chemicals that sanitize and oxidize the impurities. If the water becomes too alkaline, algae grows faster. If it becomes too acidic, sanitizers dissipate more quickly; high acidity also damages the shell finish and corrodes equipment and fittings. For these reasons, following a regular maintenance routine to keep the water balanced and to check for early signs of damage or deterioration is even more essential in spas than in pools—particularly if you plan to use your spa more than you use your pool.

Testing and treating

The same test kits used for pools (see page 83) also work well for testing the water in spas and hot tubs. Some spas come with built-in electronic testing devices that include a digital readout panel. If your unit has no built-in tester, you can get a tester kit from your spa dealer. As with pools, the water in a spa needs to maintain a pH reading between 7.2 and 7.8. Readings below 7.2 indicate excess acidity; readings above 7.8 indicate excess alkalinity. To reduce acidity, add baking soda or soda ash to the water. To reduce alkalinity, add muriatic acid. The amount you add depends on the size (capacity in gallons) of your spa or hot tub.

Chemical sanitizers commonly used in spas and hot tubs include chlorine and bromine. Bromine is considered best suited for spas and hot tubs because it's more stable in hot water and doesn't irritate skin or eyes like cholorine. However, it is less stable than chlorine in direct sunlight; if your spa or tub is outdoors, chlorine may be the better choice. Another option, ultraviolet light, works particularly well in hot water, but UV sanitizers don't oxidize (burn up) dead bacteria, so some amount of chlorine or

Below: Support equipment for a drop-in spa unit is called a skid pack. It includes a filter, a heater, at least one pump, and an air blower. The skid pack must be located at least 10 feet away from the spa, on a solid base that's at the same elevation as the top of the spa. If it's outdoors, it must be protected from weather in well-ventilated housing and easily accessible for routine maintenance.

bromine is still necessary. Because it reduces the amount of chemical needed by about 90 percent, sanitizing with UV pays benefits in the long run.

When adding chemicals to a spa, turn off the pump circuit first and never pour the chemicals into the water close to the skimmer. Concentrated doses of chemicals can damage the fabric in the filter's cartridges. Instead, pour on the far side of the spa, stirring gently with a wood paddle to distribute the chemicals. Then turn on the pump and let it run 4 to 6 hours; do another test to see if the water is in balance.

Besides pathogens (bacteria and algae), the water in a spa or hot tub contains various dissolved solids—residues and debris that gradually accumulate as you use the unit. Excess solids trigger increased alkalinity, which in turn causes shell damage and generates health hazards.

Adding chemicals won't take care of this problem; the only way to rid the unit of dissolved solids is to drain it, refilling with fresh water. (Never use water that has been run through a water-softening system; soft water is too alkaline for use in hot tubs, spas, or pools.) To determine if it's time to drain and refill, take a sample of water to your spa service technician and have it tested. The frequency of testing varies with the size of the unit, frequency of use, and number of people using it. Most units need draining and refilling once or twice a year.

Before draining your unit the first time, check with local health or environmental authorities to learn about regulations. In most communities, it's against the law to drain water containing chemical sanitizers into the storm sewers or onto the ground. Also, if your home's drains empty into a septic system, you need to empty your spa or hot tub gradually, over a period of two or three days. Emptying all the water at once could overwhelm the system and flush sludge out of the septic tank into the drainage field, clogging the laterals and causing the system to back up.

Cleaning and checking

Check your spa or hot tub daily. Potential trouble spots include the filter, the water pump and air-blower motors, the shell (particularly along the waterline), and the water itself. Most spas—and most tubs with jets—have cartridge filters. To check the cartridges, turn off the power source at the electrical panel, then remove the tank cover on the filter and inspect. If cartridges are clogged, follow the manufacturer's instructions to clean them or replace them with new ones. With power off, check the vents in the enclosure that houses the pump motors to make sure air is circulating through them freely (heat buildup is a common cause of pump failure). Check the water heater (if it's a gas-fired unit) to see if the pilot light is burning steadily, and check pipe joints for possible leaks. At least once a year, have the heating coils checked by a technician for scale deposits and corrosion.

The shell needs regular cleaning with a nonabrasive cleanser and a sponge or soft cloth. Also, use a vacuum wand (available from the dealer) to remove debris from the bottom, and a long-handled net to scoop out debris on the water's surface. After draining the unit, thoroughly clean the entire shell and add a coat of specially formulated heat- and chemical-resistant wax (also from the dealer) before refilling. (For tile- or stone-surfaced spas, use special cleaners.) For wood hot tubs or spas with wood skirting exposed to the elements, rub preservative oil into the wood two or three times a year.

For many people, the key advantage of owning a spa or hot tub is being able to retreat from the tensions of everyday life. Immersing themselves in a pool of hot, bubbling water makes the workaday world suddenly seem very far away. To heighten this effect, some spa enthusiasts beat a literal retreat—to the far reaches of their backyards or wherever they can come closest to achieving total privacy and seclusion. Although not as accessible as an indoor spa and less likely to offer a full complement of creature comforts, a backyard hideaway offers unique perks well worth considering, particularly if you put a premium on privacy and enjoy close contact with nature.

These examples illustrate several characteristics that can be incorporated into the design of any outdoor spa location to enhance the away-from-it-all feeling. For instance, although the spa pictured is situated less than 50 feet from the house, it feels more remote because it lies beyond a landscaped berm and at the end of a curving path. Also, it perches on the edge of a river, nestled among large boulders. In a low-key sense, it is a destination; when there, you're in a place separate from the rest of the yard and the world. Using similar elements, you could create a destination spa site in your own yard. A few strategically placed shrubs or trees, a raised planter, a small pond or waterfall, or even a few large plantings of ornamental grasses might be all you need to establish a subtle sense of separation and arrival. Destinations are important elements in formal landscaping too. Locating a spa at the far end of a long, straight path flanked by columnar trees or shrubs makes it seem like an outdoor room at the end of a hall. Framing it with a classic arch or a pair of urns adds to the effect by creating an entrance.

WINTERIZING YOUR SPA OR HOT TUB

If your spa will be outdoors in a cold climate and not in use for part of the winter, take precautions to protect it. Winterizing procedures vary depending on the region. Before attempting to winterize your unit, check with your dealer regarding proper procedures for your unit and your region.

- Either keep the spa filled and heated above 70 degrees F or drain it halfway and run the circulation system constantly to prevent freezing.
- Insulate the shell, the cover, and support equipment, making sure equipment is properly vented if it is kept running.
- Add antifreeze to the pipes or lower the water level until the pipes are drained.
- Dispose of all chemicals and test kit reagents. Store acids and soda ash in watertight containers.
- Remove pumps and filter cartridges; clean and take indoors.

Right: A ring of large boulders creates a sense of enclosure for the spa's sitting area. The rocks form a retaining wall for one side of the berm and also double as perches for drying off or stretching out in the sun.

Besides establishing a sense of arrival and separation, a backyard spa retreat can envelop you with a soothing sense of seclusion. In this example, seclusion is achieved by including a low landscaped berm between the spa and the yard. Lush beds of perennials growing on the berm provide just enough height and density to block views of the spa from the porch or the lawn. Again, similar elements—a row of shrubs or bushes, a vine-covered pergola, a lattice privacy screen, or a gazebo-style spa enclosure—could be used to create the same effect,.

What some might consider the major drawback of an away-from-it-all spa site—the lack of creature comforts—is seen by others as its main virtue. For hard-core enthusiasts, soaking in the open air while surrounded with natural greenery or the sounds of a brook, or while gazing up at countless constellations of stars in a wintry night sky, more than makes up for any extra inconveniences or hardships. The rustic simplicity of such settings becomes part of the escape, and the settings themselves are often designed and accessorized accordingly.

In the example shown here, candles supply the lighting, flat boulders and a wicker rocker serve as seating, and the landscaping is mostly groundcovers and grasses. The spa is a self-contained portable unit with natural wood skirting. Because all the support equipment is built in, all it requires is a firm, level concrete pad (at least 4 inches thick) and an electrical outlet (on a 110-volt, 20-amp dedicated circuit) with a ground-fault circuit interrupter. The concrete steps tinted to match the pad do double duty as a low table for drinks and towels.

Above: A low berm planted with lilies, grasses, and fragrant groundcovers forms a visual buffer for this simple outdoor spa. Although only a short stroll from the house, the spa feels more private here than it would if it were located near the back porch.

Conventional strenuous exercises, such as jogging and weight lifting, may do more harm than good because they put great stress on bones and connective tissue. These body parts take a long time to heal once injured and tend to become chronic trouble spots. Water aerobics, on the other hand, give muscles a good workout without giving the rest of the body a hammering. Exercising in water can be done in either a pool or a spa, but the most versatile option is a swim-spa.

The swim-spa pictured has been designed to accommodate various types of aerobic activities and also to serve as a conventional hydrotherapy spa and a family recreational facility. Unlike conventional spas, this swim-spa varies in depth from 36 to 46 inches, allowing room at the deep end for aerobic leg exercises or swimming in place while users soak at the shallow end. A stone bench lines the perimeter, providing a place to rest between exercises or to relax and chat with someone working out. This unit is a custom-built spa with a free-form shape to complement the curved landscaping. Installed partially above ground inside a skirting of stacked stone, the stone is capped with bullnose bricks to form a wide ledge for sitting down and swinging in or out of the water easily. A remote control panel inside the house lets the family adjust the water temperature before they go outside to use the spa. (For water aerobics, the recommended temperature range is 83 to 88 degrees F—slightly cooler than body temperature and quite a bit cooler than the range recommended for soaking and hydromassage, which is 100 to 104 degrees F.) When the spa isn't in use, it serves as an attractive reflecting pool for the rear terrace.

Right: If you're planning to use your spa for exercise, it will have to be deep enough for the water to come up to shoulder depth when you're standing upright. To increase the intensity of your water workout, add weights specifically designed for use in water.

If you don't plan on entertaining large groups in your backyard and are concerned about the long-term effects of conventional exercise or if you simply have very little space to spare for aquatic activities at home, you may want to consider installing a swim-spa instead of a pool/spa combo. Even a custom-designed unit like this one, with the extra depth at one end and a unique, naturalistic shape, will be less expensive than a custom-built pool and spa. Some of the money you save could be used to purchase handy amenities such as the indoor control panel or a collection of aerobic fitness accessories. And you could save additional money in the future by canceling your family's membership at the local health club.

Above and left: The swim-spa repeats the curves in the backyard landscaping. The spa measures about 9 × 14 feet—less than half the length of a pool—so there is room left for a terrace and porch even though the yard is fairly shallow.

The Urge to Splurge

Boost the livability of your pool or spa by including a few special design features or product upgrades in your long-range plan.

Once the design of your pool or spa comes into sharper focus and you've nailed down the cost of the basic package, it's time to compile a list of amenities that you may be able to include either right away or down the road. If you've done a good job of planning up to this point, your new pool or spa will become an important focus of family activities several months of the year—or maybe even year-round.

Investing in some well-chosen perks can pay big dividends by making your at-home aquatic playground more attractive, more fun-oriented, and more convenient to use. Choosing which upgrades to tag as must-haves won't be easy, however; the possibilities are almost endless, and designers and manufacturers introduce exciting new upgrades and options every year. Some innovations are high-tech and quite expensive; others are just simple embellishments that will fit almost any budget. Start by looking through the possibilities in this chapter to get a feel for what's available and what will best suit your family's leisure lifestyle.

An outdoor shower provides a convenient place to clean up before and after taking a dip or a sunbath and keeps the water in the pool or spa clean longer. Tucked under the eaves on a pool terrace, this handsome design is sheltered from the wind yet offers bathers a sweeping view of nearby hills and the sea.

Shady Retreats

Steady doses of warm sunshine feel great when you're in the water or stretched out on a chaise to work on your tan, but some poolside activities require a cool respite from heat and glare. As you compile a list of must-have upgrades for your pool master plan, save a place at the top of your list for some type of buyable or buildable feature that provides partial or total protection from direct sun.

The simplest option is a large patio umbrella or awning, which can be unrolled or unfolded during the sunniest part of the day and stowed in the evening and at the end of the season. These work best when all you need is a small circle of shade for two or three people or—as in the case of a large-size awning—when you can attach it directly to the house. If you know you'll be spending considerable time near the pool when that part of the yard is in full sun (or if the whole family will be congregating there for dining, lounging, conversation, and entertaining friends), a permanent shade structure will prove more practical. Not only is a permanent structure more durable, but it also offers virtually limitless design flexibility.

As the examples shown here illustrate, a shade structure can be either attached to the house or freestanding, level with the pool deck or raised on a terrace or platform, totally roofed or partly open to the sky, supported by posts or columns or by garden walls. Common examples include gazebos, cabanas, porches, and pergolas. Many shade structures are available as assemble-it-yourself kits or as project plans you can order by mail or on the Internet. Even if you prefer a custom-designed structure, it's fairly easy to build one yourself or have an experienced carpenter do the work for you.

Design pointers

To a large extent, your pool site and your family's leisure lifestyle should dictate the design you pick, but there are basic guidelines to keep in mind as you shop for plans or sketch ideas on paper. First, the overall dimensions (length, width, and height) should be generous. It's easy to underestimate how much room you need to seat a large group at a dining table or to accommodate several lounge chairs comfortably. Many gazebos, for example, are big enough to seat six or eight at a table but feel quite crowded with more than three lounge chairs and a couple of side tables. If you need casual seating for a group, avoid square or round structures, which tend to make arranging furniture loosely and getting in and out difficult.

Second, the roof and walls of the structure should be designed to temper the sun, not simply blot it out altogether. The object is to create just the right amount of shade, not to build a dark, cavelike enclosure. Unless you live in a very warm, humid climate, sitting in deep shade while wearing damp swimsuits can be chilly, especially in a steady breeze.

Third, carefully consider the pros and cons of the location of the structure. If you don't plan to have an outdoor kitchen (see pages 112–113) near the pool, a shade structure that's part of a deck or terrace adjoining the house, with easy access to the indoor kitchen, may be a good choice. An attached deck or terrace is usually a few

Below: The elegantly trimmed, egg-crate design of this shade structure works well as a freestanding pavilion. It perches on a deck that holds a table, chairs, and large potted plants.

Left: A low-maintenance redwood trellis tops this classically designed shade structure. The generous dimensions and rectangular shape of the structure allow ample room for dining and for traffic between the house and the pool.

steps above the pool area and, therefore, offers a good vantage point for observing activities in and near the water. On the other hand, steps always pose a safety hazard, especially if people walk up and down them in bare feet and dripping-wet swimsuits. Placing a shade structure next to the pool or spa gives you the option of eliminating steps. It will also direct traffic that otherwise tends to go through the house.

Finally, choose a design that lends itself to low-maintenance materials. Airy, suntempering structures such as trellis-topped pergolas and lattice-paneled gazebos and porches make charming places to hang out and keep cool, but they can become prob-

lems when it comes time to scrape, sand, and repaint all those crisscrossing strips of exposed wood. Fortunately, trellises and lattice panels are now available in no-paint, rigid polymer, as are railings, porch columns, decorative brackets, lap and shingle siding, and other structural and decorative components for outdoor construction. If you prefer the authenticity of real wood, consider treating it with stains or weathering oils rather than paint. That way, the finish doesn't blister and crack as it ages, and when you need to give it a fresh coat, no sanding is necessary to achieve a good bond.

Falling Water

Above: This large site-built waterfall includes a grotto, large boulders, and a reef. It provides an attractive focal point and offers swimmers a quiet hideway with places to perch and take a sunbath. A wide ledge spreads the waterfall into a curtain of rivulets at the entrance to the grotto.

Right: The pool in this urban yard features a European-style waterfall. A stone-capped wall, softened by plantings, forms an arch above the gurgling waterfall, which falls continually into the pool below.

There is something uniquely inviting and soothing about the sounds and sights of falling water. Whether the source is a single jet, a multitiered cascade, or just a narrow stream trickling quietly over a bed of pebbles, the result is a pleasant serenade that calms frayed nerves and never grows tiresome. Falling water is also the perfect white noise—a natural buffer against jarring sounds that threaten to erode the peace and quiet of house and home.

Plug and play

Backyard fountains, waterfalls, and brooks were once considered extravagances that only the rich could afford—or had the room to accommodate. Fortunately, neither is true any longer. Although elaborate waterscapes are still costly and can occupy

sizeable space, it's also possible to work wonders with water on a much smaller and simpler scale. If your pool or spa area is relatively small or you're working within a tight budget, the number of options is still surprisingly varied. For example, both pools and spas can be fitted with retractable fountain jets that telescope into the bottom when not in use. Another option is a fountain that floats on the surface; when you need more room for swimming or water sports, you simply nudge it off to one side. Plug-in fountains (like the floating version) cost around $100; built-in fountains range in cost from $500 to $1,500. Waterfalls are also great space-savers; a wide, thin sheet of water emerging from a slot in the pool wall requires practically no horizontal square footage yet generates robust sound. Small waterfalls, available as accessory items for pools and spas, cost approximately $300.

If, on the other hand, you have room for something more elaborate, you might want a multitiered fountain, a series of arc-shape jets, or a full-size naturalistic waterfall. Many pool and spa manufacturers offer fancy fountains and jets as accessory or upgrade options, and at least one company

sells a programmable fountain, complete with digital software for creating your own dancing water show—including music and lighting. It's also possible to buy prefabricated synthetic stone components that you assemble to create a naturalistic boulder-strewn cascade and poolside grotto.

There are practical considerations to keep in mind if you plan to add a special water feature to your pool or spa area. First, you need to boost the circulation system's pumping capacity, especially if the new feature is a large fountain or waterfall. Switching to a larger pump is not usually the best way to do this because pumps need to be hydraulically balanced with the other components in the system. A better solution is to add a second pump close to the water feature itself. Second, you need to provide electrical power near the feature to run the pump and/or any accessory features such as music or lighting. Third, you need to test and treat the water more often because waterfalls and fountains increase evaporation of treated water, which can throw the water out of balance. How often to test and treat will depend on whether you run the water feature only at certain times or continuously.

Above: Although the house next door is just a few feet away, the stone wall on this pool works as an effective sight and sound buffer—as well as an eye-catching design element. Pool water recirculates to form a series of small waterfalls on one side of the pool.

Poolside Cooking and Serving

Below: This poolside grill area tucks under the eave along one side of a rear dining terrace. In addition to a built-in gas grill, it features several storage compartments topped with a rugged poured-concrete countertop, which doubles as a buffet server for the table.

Feeling as if you're on vacation in your own backyard is much easier if your pool or spa area is equipped with its own refreshment bar or outdoor kitchen. With everything you need for serving beverages, snacks, or short-order meals just a few steps from the water's edge, you can spend the whole day in your swim togs, soaking up the sun and fresh air. An outdoor bar or kitchen saves trips to the house, cutting down on wear and tear in your indoor kitchen. It also makes it easy for everyone, guests as well as family, to pitch in or help themselves, giving you more time to enjoy the water.

Keep it simple

Because outdoor cooking and serving tend to be very informal, the facility itself can be quite simple and compact compared to a regular kitchen. If your budget is slim or if you prefer to work in stages, you can gain convenience by adding just a countertop and some undercounter storage, especially if you already have an outdoor grill and an insulated beverage cooler. The counter should be large enough to provide necessary work and serving space. Storage cabinets should be sized to accommodate the cooler, a large bottle of fresh water, at least one large trash can, barbecue tools, bags of briquettes or a spare propane tank, cleanup supplies, and disposable plates, tumblers, and eating utensils.

Electrical power should run from the house to an all-weather GFCI outlet mounted on the base cabinet to plug in countertop appliances. In later stages you could add either a dry or wet sink, an undercounter refrigerator or icemaker, a built-in gas grill, and a trellised canopy. If you live in a cold climate, however, keep in mind that refrigerators and freezers must be

Right: This U-shape poolside kitchen is recessed partly below ground to accommodate swim-up seating. It's equipped with a large, built-in grill, undercounter refrigerator, glazed ceramic tile countertop, and a Polynesian-style canopy. Outdoor lighting in the canopy makes it easy to use the kitchen after dark and lends a festive air for parties and holidays.

moved indoors in the wintertime; operating
such devices at temperatures below 40
degrees F can cause permanent damage to
the cooling system.

Because outdoor kitchens are fairly
compact, they fit virtually anywhere. For a
basic layout, all you need is a space
measuring approximately 2×5 feet. For
larger kitchens—ones with several built-in
appliances and a sink—you may want to
add a peninsula at one end to form an L-
shape layout. Or close in the work area to
form a U-shape layout, and use part of it as a
counter for serving.

Pick tough finishes

When choosing finish materials, look for
products that weather well and offer extra
protection against—or camouflage for—
chips and stains. When cooking, serving,
and dining outdoors, spills are inevitable.
The foods and beverages often served outdoors, such as hamburgers, hot dogs, grilled
chicken, and carbonated drinks, tend to
leave stubborn stains when handled care-
lessly. If the floor of your kitchen area will
be covered with porous pavers, such as
bricks or Mexican tiles, it should be properly sealed. If your countertop will be
surfaced with glazed ceramic tile, avoid
using pure white grout; medium or charcoal
gray may prove much more practical.

Right: A gas-fired ground-level fire pit creates a dramatic focal point in the pool area at night. Its proximity to the spa, the pool, and the deck means that bathers can see and enjoy it no matter where they are.

Fireside Focal Points

Below: The rustic redwood pergola and hillside landscaping help define sitting and dining space near the fireplace beside this pool/spa. A retaining wall doubles as a raised hearth and built-in bench. Rough-textured white stucco on the fireplace and chimney also covers the outdoor kitchen and the sides of the spa.

In many locales, temperatures often dip sharply once the sun drops near the horizon, making poolside lounging a bit uncomfortable whether the pool itself is heated or not. Yet evenings may be the only part of the day when you have ample time to hang out at the pool with family and friends. Also, some locales that have balmy summer evenings have relatively short summers bracketed by several weeks of mild spring and fall weather warm enough for swimming in a heated pool but too chilly for sitting outdoors in wet suits. One way to put some extra flexibility in your poolside routine is to include a hearth area in your master plan.

A wealth of choices

Like many of the other amenities discussed in this chapter, outdoor hearth options are available to suit practically any budget, style preference, and space requirement. Perhaps the simplest and most affordable is a freestanding metal wood burner, which needs no chimney yet resembles a four-sided wood-burning fireplace. Metal wood burners, sometimes called patio fireplaces, are available at discount home centers for less than $100.

Another fairly simple option is a fire pit—a raised or sunken area lined with stones, bricks, or sand. Usually site-built, fire pits are designed either as wood burners or as open-flame gas burners (fueled with natural or propane gas piped from the home's main line). Fire pits vary in cost depending on how much skilled labor is needed to construct the pit and install the fuel source.

Other inexpensive options include a gas-fired, portable campfire (its ceramic logs resemble rustic kindling) and a barbecue unit that converts to a hearth after the meal is cooked (the firebox is enclosed with glass walls similar to those of a built-in fireplace). Portable units, available at hearth products showrooms, cost from $100 to $1,000.

If you have room in your pool area—and your budget—for a full-scale built-in fireplace, another range of options opens up, with prices varying from a few hundred dollars to several thousand. Do you prefer a gas-fired unit or a wood burner? A prefabricated metal unit or a site-built masonry unit? A raised hearth or one flush with the pool deck or the floor of the lounge area? Will a firebox open on one side work best for your situation, or will a two-, three-, or four-sided unit be more practical? If your lounge adjoins the house, should the fireplace share the same chimney as your indoor fireplace or should the two fireplaces instead be one unit, with a two-way firebox? Selection of finishes also involves a spectrum of options—for the unit itself and for the surround. Most prefab units are available in a matte black finish designed to complement masonry, stucco, or wood surrounds. At

least one manufacturer also offers outdoor fireplaces with stainless-steel fronts for a stylish and durable contemporary look. In general, you should finish the surround to match or harmonize with your pool-deck or shade-structure finishes so it becomes an integral part of the design.

Once you've zeroed in on a particular hearth unit, consider other features you want in your hearth area. If you've chosen a wood burner, you may also want a large compartment for storing wood. If you plan to host large gatherings, consider installing built-in seating to supplement lounge furniture. If your pool area gets windy at night, you may need a canopy or wind screen, and if the nights are usually clear you might want to make the canopy transparent so you can still gaze up at the stars while you relax by the fire. One easy way to do this is to install large skylights in the roof.

Above: The hearth area for this backyard pool tucks into a jog in the home's exterior, offering privacy and protection from chilly breezes. The raised hearth provides built-in seating, and the glass roof lets in warm sun and allows views of the stars on clear nights.

Natural Perks

It's customary to think of a swimming pool as something apart from nature, an artificial, streamlined alternative to the proverbial old swimming hole, the seashore, or the sandy-bottom lake where you had a picnic on the 4th of July. But lately, back-yard pools have begun to resemble their natural counterparts more and more. You no longer have to settle for a pool configuration that's basically just a large tank surrounded by flat pavement; instead, you can create the illusion of a natural body of water, complete with many of the features that made outings at the lake or the seashore so memorable.

One such feature is the beach entry. Instead of vertical walls on all four sides of the pool, one side ramps down gradually into the water just like a natural beach would, making it easy for bathers to get in and out of the water and providing a place to sit in shallow water to rest or sunbathe. To enhance the natural effect—and to ensure safe footing—beach entries are usually surfaced with a pebbly aggregate or a sandlike texture. A pool with a beach entry costs approximately $1,500 to $2,000 more than one with conventional vertical walls.

Another naturalistic feature is the disappearing or infinity edge. Walls in conventional pools form a continuous lip above the waterline, creating a visual boundary. In an infinity-edge pool, at least one wall ends just below the waterline, creating the illusion that the water surface extends to the horizon just as the surface of a large lake or an ocean does. To enhance the effect, the water that flows over the wall is captured and recirculated unobtrusively,

Below: This rock-bordered pool has a natural, boulder-strewn look, complete with a reef submerged just a few inches below the water level. Another reef is the ledge where the waterfall enters the pool. These reefs offer spots for sunbathing or dangling feet without being completely submerged in the water.

making the water appear to drift or flow into the distance. Infinity-edge pools require considerable technical know-how and on-site construction and can add anywhere from $10,000 to $100,000 to the cost of a pool, depending on how many edges are involved, how steep the site is, and how complex the pool shape is. (For more information, see pages 44-45).

A third type of natural feature frequently found in today's pools is the reef. A reef is any large platform submerged a few inches below the water surface to provide a place for lounging or sunbathing between swims. Some reefs are long, bench-like shapes that line the sides of the pool; others are extra-wide or extra-deep steps, or irregularly shaped ledges. They may nestle between boulders along the edge of the pool or project beneath or behind waterfalls. Including a simple bench-shaped reef adds about $300 to the cost of a pool, but more complex designs may cost from $800 to $1,000.

Above: The infinity edge on this pool makes the surface appear to merge with the lake below. Dark-color aggregate disguises the pool walls beneath the water's surface, heightening the illusion that the pool water meets the lake water.

High-Tech Helpers

The more your pool or spa takes care of itself, the more time you have to relax and enjoy it. Many time- and labor-saving devices have been developed to make this possible, with new devices being introduced every year. Although some are relatively simple, low-cost items available for a few dollars at your hardware store or discount home center, most are sophisticated, high-tech devices with hefty price tags. Whether you have room in your budget for splurges of this type or need to put them off until you can upgrade, buying some extra quality time by the pool may prove well worth the additional expense.

Automated aids

One way to put your money to work is to invest in an automated control system. Choices range from simple, inexpensive timers for regulating pumps or outdoor lighting, to all-encompassing programmable master control systems that regulate not only your pool pumps and lighting but also its valves, heater, alarm system, cleaning components, and water treatment system. Some versions are hardwired; others are primarily wireless. Low-voltage lighting timers cost as little as $20; a master control system, complete with a remote touch-pad panel (usually installed indoors) and/or a remote module, costs about $2,500. You can also get individual components that perform certain tasks automatically, such as robotic pool cleaners, which prowl around the bottom or sides of the pool and suck up dirt and debris. Some robotic cleaners are battery-powered; others run on a long power cord. Robotic cleaners cost between $1,000 and $4,000. A less-expensive option—one that scoops up small particles of dirt and debris—is a long, snakelike vacuum hose that plugs directly into the pool skimmer inlet. This cleaner costs about $700.

If you lack the time or flexibility in your daily schedule to treat your pool water by hand, you can relegate this task to an automatic chemical feeder or generator. Automatic ozone and chlorine generators sense when the water is out of balance and add ozone or chlorine molecules as needed. Ozone generators cost about $1,000; chlorine generators are about $1,500. Also, you can cut back on routine maintenance chores by investing in high-grade equipment components. One type is a 1-horsepower pump made of lightweight nylon and plastic parts. Impervious to the chemicals in pool water, nylon and plastic parts are more durable than metal ones and also quieter-running. The cost for this new breed of pump is about $500.

Pool safety devices have gone high-tech too. For example, if you have an above-ground pool, you can get an alarm system with an in-home remote receiver for only $60. Remote receivers are also available for inground pool alarms. For optimum safety and peace of mind, you can equip your pool with an automated pool cover, which unrolls or retracts at the touch of a button and can support the weight of several adults when unrolled. Prices for automated covers vary from $6,000 to $10,000, depending on your pool size and shape.

POOL & SPA POINTERS

With an electric-powered cover, closing a pool is a cinch. It glides on recessed tracks under the pool coping and rolls up into a housing at one end. Cost varies from $6,000 to $10,000 depending on the size and shape of the pool.

Safety covers, which can support the weight of several people, cost significantly more but work the same way. To know if a cover has this higher level of safety, look for an ASTM rating; without it, the cover is *not* safe for anyone to stand on.

Another high-tech feature to consider is a plug-and-play control panel. You can control 32 different pool-area features from up to 300 feet away, including the pump, heater, valves, fountains, lights, and spa jets. Cost: about $1,000.

Equipped with fiber-optic lighting, this pool becomes an eye-catching light sculpture after the sun goes down. Flexible plastic tubing pipes the light around and under the pool surface from a single light source, eliminating the need for multiple fixtures and bulbs. Cost varies from $1,000 to $5,000 depending on the area and the number of features illuminated.

Light shows

If you plan to entertain frequently by the pool or simply want your pool or spa to be a major focal point after dark, check out the latest advances in outdoor lighting. Dramatic breakthroughs in light-source (lamp) technology make it possible to decorate your poolscape with glowing bands of color and even change the color of the water itself—all at the touch of a button.

Three technologies in particular—LED, SAm, and fiber optics—have proven especially versatile. LED (light-emitting diode) lamps are about the same size as ordinary floodlight lamps but use only a fraction as much wattage and generate much less heat to produce the same light intensity (15 watts versus 150). Also, when linked to a digital programming component (such as your home computer), a single LED lamp can mix all three primary colors—red, yellow, and blue—in varying combinations to produce a light show. SAm fixtures (an abbreviation for Spectrum Amerlite) contain two quartz halogen lamps and a rotating color wheel linked by electronic circuitry; by touching a button, you can make the light—and your pool or spa water—run through a whole spectrum of vivid colors. Fiber optics use flexible fiberglass tubing to pipe white or colored light from a single intense source (usually a 150-watt metal halide lamp) to wherever you want it, such as around the pool perimeter, in the pool water, under step treads or fountain sprays, and inside a cascading waterfall. Because all the light issues from just one lamp tucked out of sight near the pool area, you not only use less wattage to illuminate a large area, you also eliminate the hazard of having hardwired light sockets near water (fiber optic tubing carries only light, not electric current, so it's non-conductive).

As you might expect, these new lighting options are expensive. One LED or SAm lamp costs $600; costs for fiber optic systems vary from $1,000 to $5,000, depending on the size of the area and the number of features being lighted. However, each option uses a lamp that lasts longer than conventional lightbulbs. And giving your pool or spa a festive air for parties and holidays or turning it into a scenic backdrop for your indoor living space with just a flick of a switch will leave you more time to just sit back and enjoy it all.

An Outdoor Room

Opposite top: Family-friendly features in this poolscape include comfortable lounging areas, two dining alcoves, and a generous pool and spa. Wide, bullnose ledges rimming the pool and spa are the right height for kids to sit and dry off or dangle their feet in the water.

Below: Along one side of the pool, three small waterfalls cascade from narrow slots in the rock wall. The musical sound of the falling water is a soothing tension reliever, and children love playing beneath the water too.

One sure way to get maximum benefit from your backyard aquatic playground is turn your entire yard into one big outdoor room, a kind of open-air great-room, with multiple areas to serve various activities simultaneously. That's the idea behind the poolscape pictured here, which fills a 2,500-square-foot yard in a compact subdivision. Although neighboring houses stand just five feet from the lot line on two sides, strategically placed garden walls, shade structures, and greenery define the room's boundaries and give it the feel of a resort.

Each feature of the design is geared toward family-oriented fun and relaxation. The pool's elongated rectangular shape creates a large stretch of open water for games or swimming laps, and the integral spa at one end provides a place for parents to unwind and supervise or for kids to warm up when they get chilled. Wide bullnose coping on the pool and spa offers places to perch, while a series of three waterfalls at one end make it extra fun to splash around.

When the family works up an appetite, they can head for the fully equipped outdoor kitchen and serving bar, which lies just a few steps from the spa. Two pergola-shaded dining areas flank the kitchen, offering ample seating space when relatives and friends stop by.

As you develop the master plan for your pool or spa area, think about which features you can include if you converted your own backyard into an outdoor great-room. Activities that your family already enjoys indoors may offer useful hints. For example, if fireside conversations are a favorite way to spend time together at your house, you may want to consider including a hearth area in your outdoor room too. If big Sunday breakfasts are a long-standing tradition, you may want to equip your outdoor kitchen with a built-in grill and refrigerator so you can continue this activity in a casual setting throughout the pool season. And if your house is often the one chosen for big family get-togethers, you may want to look for ways to incorporate extra seating and dining space near the pool with extra storage space in the outdoor kitchen or bar area.

Above and left: The outdoor kitchen features a built-in grill and a hardy poured-concrete countertop that stairsteps to form a serving bar. The bar hides kitchen clutter yet the cook still has a clear view of the pool, spa, and sitting areas. Tawny ledger stone cladding unifies the main features.

Backyard Bali-Hai

Stepping into this backyard pool retreat in Florida is like being transported to a private island in the South Seas—without the intervening hassles of packing your bags and enduring long hours in a plane. As you meander around the pool under a lacy canopy of intertwining palm fronds and soak up the sounds of cascading water, it's hard to believe that this little paradise sits on a postage-stamp corner lot at the intersection of two busy streets and that a few years ago the tiny backyard was bare ground.

Because of its location, this poolscape is purposely designed to create a strong sense of enclosure and retreat. Layers of lush greenery form a natural privacy wall on two sides, and the house and garage complete the enclosure on the other two. You would think the yard's diminutive size (barely 50 square feet) would rule out an outdoor living area as elaborate as this, but it has proved a boon; it's easier and less expensive to achieve a total sense of enclosure—and thus the illusion of total escape.

Clever design also plays a key role. Giving the pool a free-form shape and placing it on a diagonal axis makes it appear larger than its actual dimensions. Along its curvy perimeter, the pool deck winds in and out of the dense greenery, forming little mini-getaways that overlook the pool yet feel separate and insular. One harbors an umbrella table with seating for three or four; another offers the solitary pleasure of stretching out in a hammock. Special areas adjoining other sides of the pool include an elevated, boulder-rim spa and a trellis-roof outdoor kitchen. The spa is equipped with its own mini "fireplace"—a rustic Mexican chimenea.

Although the locale and the theme of this design are tropical—inspired by vacation trips to Hawaii and the Mexican Riviera—the concept of a total-enclosure outdoor pool area could be adapted to almost any theme, especially if your yard is small or if a portion of it can be enclosed easily with a natural or artificial boundary. One tactic is to ring the yard with fast-growing trees or shrubs. Another is to build a high garden wall. A third is to erect a series of arbors, pergolas, and trellises and plant fast-growing vines to train across them. Also, if you

Right: This backyard pool area brings the South Seas close to home with a palm-fringed tropical garden; a rippling, pale blue pool; a Robinson Crusoe hammock; and a spa that seems to be bubbling out of a lava-rock fissure.

Opposite below left: Grilling hotcakes and sausages by the pool on Sunday mornings is a treat rather than a task, thanks to the well-equipped outdoor galley. Part of the U-shape work area tucks under the eaves of the house; the rest curves beneath a broad redwood trellis. Slats in the trellis mimic the rhythmic lines of the palm fronds.

Left: Nestled between two palm trees, a hammock is a comfortable spot for an afternoon of reading or even a siesta.

Below right: Overflow from the spa spills across a layer of flat stones mortared into the coping to duplicate the sounds of a natural waterfall. Behind the spa, a Mexican chimenea—a small freestanding fireplace made of terra-cotta— provides welcome warmth on chilly evenings.

plan to include small buildings, consider placing them where they can be linked to one another and to existing structures (such as the house and garage) by means of lattice-screened fences or trellised walkways so that all elements work together as a privacy screen and an outer boundary for the room.

Wet, Wild, and Wonderful

Whimsy is a large part of the charm that draws people to such popular vacation getaways as the Caribbean, the South Seas, and various family-oriented theme parks. Escaping to a place that lets you feel like a kid again can be a very effective tonic for the stresses of everyday life. Trekking to an exotic travel destination each year is one way to revisit your youth, but you can also do it much faster in your own backyard—by giving the pool or spa area a decidedly whimsical spin.

That was the aim behind this poolscape. It was designed for a family with three teenage sons and frequent overnight guests. The entire backyard was turned into a water-oriented theme park, with a strong emphasis on fun. Many elements that create a playful mood at vacation meccas are here too: Bold splashes of color enliven traditional architectural forms; offbeat shapes and patterns evoke younger years; an unusual palette of finish materials adds sparkle and sheen where least expected; and of course a central activity area—in this case, the pool and spa—to experience the simple joy of being a kid again. The oval, 18×36-foot pool wraps around an elevated spa equipped with a two-speed bubbler—one speed is extra-high for wild-water action. Spillover from the spa forms several waterfalls around the rim.

Behind the spa, a bright yellow poolhouse with trellised porch contains a food and beverage serving area, with casement windows that open to form a pass-through snack bar. In warm weather, a large striped awning reminiscent of cabana tents at the seashore drapes across the trellis. Matching awning-stripe cushions pad the chaises on the pool deck.

Below: Bright colors, funky furniture, and friendly architecture set the mood for fun in this backyard. The sunny poolhouse performs multiple roles: concession stand, cabana, entertainment center, and guest suite. The generous spa features glass-block walls faced with tiles with photo-transfer images of river rock. Slim slabs of granite cap the glass blocks, which stop at water level for spillover to cascade into the pool.

Left: An outdoor shower mounted on the side of the poolhouse provides an easy and quick way to wash off dirt and chlorine after a hard day's fun in the pool. Pavers under the showerhead include bricks set into squares of raised-tread industrial metal flooring.

Below: The pool shell and pool steps are finished with a pebbly blue coating that contains crystalline flecks. The pebbly texture provides good traction for bare feet, and the crystalline particles sparkle in the sun. Diamond-shapes cut from the photo-transfer tiles are inlaid on each step and bordered with a row of jewel-toned pebbles.

Hidden helpers

Like any cleverly engineered theme park, this one includes many high-tech helpers that integrate unobtrusively in the design to generate extra dimensions of fun—and eliminate real world maintenance chores. Two sets of computerized controls—one in the poolhouse and one in the main house—let the owners change the waterfall settings and the color of the pool lighting. An indoor control sets temperatures in the pool and the spa. The poolhouse includes an entertainment center to pipe music underground to speakers camouflaged to resemble rocks in the pool area, and people inside the poolhouse are able to listen to music different from that playing by the pool. The pool itself is virtually maintenance-free, with an automatic chlorination system, an automatic overflow control, and an automatic built-in pressure-cleaning system.

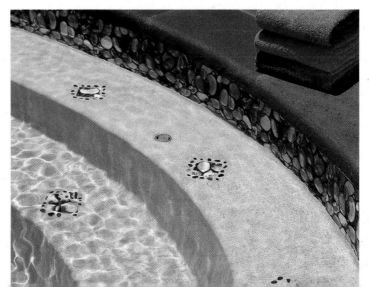

Serenity enfolds you the moment you step into this backyard pool oasis in San Diego—and once there, there's little reason to leave. If the sheer beauty of the place doesn't put you immediately at ease, there are numerous other ways to unwind. Besides the elegant tile-lined pool and integral spa, the attractions include a two-story poolhouse that's much more than just a handsome backdrop; it's also a home workout center, a wet bar, a cabana, a media center, and a guest suite. You can play a favorite CD or DVD while burning off the frustrations of the day on the weight machines, then change into swim togs, pour yourself a refreshing drink, and stretch out in the late afternoon sun on the whitewashed wood pool deck. Or take a cooling dip or swim some laps and finish off the evening in the spa.

Despite all the conveniences and high style, the setting for this poolscape is a relatively small, urban backyard. To expand the space—or create the illusion of spaciousness—the poolhouse perches on slim columns and its lower walls are partly lattice panels. Keeping the color palette light also helps push back the actual boundaries.

Designing your poolhouse as an extension or annex of your main house is a smart strategy if your lot is narrow and your house lacks certain amenities that can't be added on. Even if you live in a cold climate, a poolhouse can earn its keep year-round by doubling as guest quarters, a home office, a family craft and hobby center, a teen lounge, or simply bonus storage for bulky seasonal gear.

Opposite top and bottom: This poolhouse and pool are dramatic and complementary artful counterpoints. The wood plank floor extends as the pool deck; one of the side walls projects as a lattice privacy screen along the deck; and the front wall arches gracefully across the spa. The glass door on the left opens to stairs that serve the guest suite on the upper level.

Right: Beyond the spa, steps lead down to the workout area, which is equipped with a built-in media cabinet and wet bar. Lattice panels and stained-glass windows on each side of the cabinet filter the bright sun.

Index

Page numbers in **bold italic** type indicate photographs.

Credits & Resources

Thanks to the following manufacturers for supplying photographs:

Pages 10 (lower left) and 90: Endless Pools, 800-233-0741, endlesspools.com
Page 23: Crestwood Pools, Inc., 607-786-0010, crestwoodpools.com
Page 25: Ester Williams Pools, by Delair Group, 800-235-0185, delairgroup.com
Page 31: Blue Hawaii Pools, 800-393-7699, ext. 10
Page 73: Fiberstars, Inc., 800-327-7877
Page 92: HotSpring Portable Spas, 800-999-4688, hotspring.com

Thanks to the National Spa & Pool Institute for providing the following photographs:

Pages 6 (center left), 8 (top and bottom), 12, 13 (top), 24, 28, 29, 35, 36, 50, 51, 53 (top), 56, 57, 63 (top), 64, 68 (top), 69 (bottom), 72, 114 (top)